VENTRILOQUISM MADE EASY

Kolby King

This book belongs to

Winston

DOVER PUBLICATIONS, INC.
Mineola, New York

Special thanks to:

*The Maher Ventriloquist Studios for helping me as a
beginning ventriloquist; my family for supporting
me; and the Lord, who has blessed me with this
talent.*

Copyright

Bibliographical Note

Ventriloquism Made Easy is a new work, first published by Dover Publications,
Inc., in 1997.

Library of Congress Cataloging-in-Publication Data

King, Kolby.
  Ventriloquism made easy / Kolby King.
      p.   cm.
  ISBN-13: 978-0-486-29683-8 (pbk.)
  ISBN-10: 0-486-29683-0 (pbk.)
  1. Ventriloquism.   I. Title.
GV1557.K45   1997
793.8'9—dc21   96-52592
                                                                     CIP

Manufactured in the United States by LSC Communications
29683009   2020
www.doverpublications.com

Contents

1. Before You Begin

So you want to be a ventriloquist? Of course you do. If you didn't, you wouldn't be reading this book. But to get the most out of this book you must possess the desire to learn—the desire to be the best you can be, so that you may be able to master the illusion that can open your eyes to new worlds.

Allow me to begin by answering a common question: who can be a ventriloquist? The answer: anyone. At least, anyone who is willing to practice and to invest the time and energy required to develop the talent.

Ventriloquists are no more special than anyone else in the world. They aren't born with certain-shaped mouths. They aren't born with a unique ability to talk through their noses. They are no more gifted than the neighbor's dog down the street.

Some talents are natural. At birth these inherent gifts are already present, but nobody is a ventriloquist at birth. Ventriloquism is not a natural talent, but an acquired one. In other words, it's not a gift with which you are born, but one that is developed by practice and hard work.

You—*yes, you*—can be a ventriloquist.

To get the most out of this book keep a highlighter or ink pen nearby as you read. Then when you happen upon an important sentence or phrase, such as "The first and last rule of ventriloquism is: practice, practice, practice," underline it. This will help you and makes reviewing much easier. Mark anything to which you may wish to return in the future.

Take your time while reading this book. There's no reason to hurry. Stop, relax and enjoy. Review the chapters you have already read. Think about what you are reading and keep a positive attitude.

Always imagine yourself doing your best. Imagine performing before television cameras and an audience of hundreds of people. You're the entertainment, and they have focused all their attention on YOU! They're all laughing—not at you, but with you. They're rolling in the aisles. You're great. You're a hit. You're the best! The cameramen are laughing so hard that they can't hold the cameras still.

1

The television screen at home is wiggling back and forth, side to side, and the viewers are getting seasick.

But more importantly, you're comfortable and enjoying every moment. As you leave the stage the applause is deafening. People are whistling and shouting, "More! We want more!"

Sound silly? Okay, perhaps it is an exaggeration, but all things are possible.

In time you may perform on television or in front of thousands of people. You may be asked to be the entertainment at important functions and events. Your name may become very well known.

On the other hand, these may not be your goals. Many excellent ventriloquists don't have grand ambitions. They're content to develop the talent just to become better school-teachers or better counselors or chaplains. They have no desire to make money as ventriloquists. They have no desire to be famous. Their goal is simply to make a few children smile at the hospital. Or they want to warn kids to stay away from drugs. Ventriloquism can also be used in counseling children or working with the mentally challenged.

Whatever your reason is for wanting to become a ventriloquist, it's possible to attain your goals, and the extent to which you desire to use your talent will determine the extent to which you need to practice. It will also determine the types of dialogues that you will want to develop.

Regardless of your motives, always strive to become better. There's always room for improvement.

Here's an important key to remember as you read this book:

The day you stop getting better is the day you say, "I'm the best I can be."

That's worth repeating (in other words, it's time to put that highlighter to work):

The day you stop getting better is the day you say, "I'm the best I can be."

Now, let's begin our adventure into the wide world of ventriloquism.

2. Ventriloquism: The Basics

Ventriloquism is the art of speaking without moving your lips, so that speech appears to originate from another source. This creates the illusion that the ventriloquist is "throwing" his voice.

The ventriloquist does not *really* throw his voice. No one can make his voice originate from another source, but the ventriloquist creates this illusion. He is like a magician. Magicians create illusions to mystify their audiences: ventriloquists do the same. They create an illusion that makes an inanimate object, such as the *vent figure*, become alive. (*Vent figure* stands for "ventriloquist figure." Sometimes the little fellows are offended by the term "dummy.") The object appears to talk, to move and to act like a real person. It can laugh, cough, sneeze and become alive to an audience.

There are three basic keys to ventriloquism:

1. **No lip movement from the ventriloquist**
2. **The vent figure's lips move (the *distraction*)**
3. **A voice contrast between the ventriloquist and the vent figure**

An important question must be addressed before we go on: why does this illusion work? If the ventriloquist isn't throwing his voice, can't the audience hear that the sound is really coming from him?

Try a simple experiment. The next time you hear the siren of an emergency vehicle, such as a police car or a fire truck, close your eyes. Try to pinpoint the exact location of the vehicle or even the general direction from which it comes. Sometimes you come close. Other times the sound seems to come from all directions. Don't worry: you don't have hearing problems. Your ears are fine, just normal. They, like every other human ear, can't pinpoint the exact origin of the sound. With this fact, the illusion of ventriloquism has begun.

During the ventriloquist's act the human ear is not keen enough to detect the correct origin of the sound it hears and to distinguish who is really doing the talking. The mem-

3

bers of the audience will be unable to distinguish the source of the voice unless they are closer than about three or four feet.

Ventriloquism, like magic tricks, contains a distraction. This distraction is the movement of the vent figure's mouth. Since no lip movement can be seen on the ventriloquist, and the figure's mouth is moving to the words, this movement *suggests* that the sound is actually coming from the figure's mouth. Then, since the audience is unable to distinguish that the ventriloquist is really doing the talking, the vent figure *appears* to be speaking the words.

Voice contrast is the third factor that creates the ventriloquist's illusion. Obviously you and your figure shouldn't share the same voice. The greater the contrast, the better the illusion.

There are four options you can take in developing a contrasting voice. You can raise your puppet's voice, lower it, develop an accent or use a combination of the three. You can also let the figure talk at a different speed than you or allow him to make grammatical errors. As you practice throughout this book, begin to develop a puppet's voice that is comfortable for you.

Here's an important key: be sure that you don't hurt your voice by forcing it higher or lower than it should go. A proper vent figure's voice should never hurt or strain your vocal cords.

Another important key in developing a voice is to let the voice be suitable for the puppet. For example, if the puppet is a cowboy, give it an Old Southern drawl. If it is a high-society, high-class puppet, give it a proper high-society, high-class voice. If he looks like he should have a low voice, give him a low voice. If he looks like he should have a high voice, give him a high voice.

Then let that voice become a part of that puppet. Don't share it with any others. Your vent figures need to develop their own identities and their own separate personalities.

Finally, don't sacrifice lip movement in order to make your voice stretch higher or lower than it should or by trying to implement an accent. Accents are great, but not if they make your lips move. If an accent can be mastered, it will be a great benefit, but it's not worth sacrificing the overall illusion for its sake.

Also, if *you* have an accent, it will add to your performance if your vent figure does not.

These are the basics. You know them, but knowing them doesn't make you a ventriloquist. Now you must achieve them.

Be patient, though. Always be patient, because only through patience and practice can you become a good ventriloquist. Anyone can ventriloquize, but those who are really good are the ones who are patient and who apply the three major rules of becoming an excellent ventriloquist: The first rule is practice. The second rule is practice. Guess what the third rule is? That's right—practice.

Practice, practice, practice.

"Practice makes perfect." Probably not, but it will make you an outstanding ventriloquist.

A house is only as good as its foundation. This chapter is your foundation. Visit it often and review the three basics of ventriloquism:

1. **No lip movement from the ventriloquist**
2. **The vent figure's lips move (the *distraction*)**
3. **A voice contrast between the ventriloquist and the vent figure**

You're now ready to learn the secret of speaking without moving your lips!

3. The Secret: From A to Z

Welcome to the most important chapter in this book. Prepare yourself to learn the "secret" of ventriloquism. How can you speak without moving your lips? What's the trick?

There are only a few letters in the alphabet that require lip movement. All of the others can be said easily without using your lips. Speaking is the result of tongue movement, and the reason that we use our lips is to help us enunciate properly. But you, in this chapter, are going to begin to learn to speak without any lip movement whatsoever.

Speaking without lip movement led me to become a ventriloquist. When I was in the fourth grade, my teacher gave daily "assignment savers" to students who weren't *caught* talking in class. In other words, if you didn't talk during class, you wouldn't have to turn in an assignment of your choice.

So I tried to teach myself to talk without moving my lips. It's really not that difficult. By the end of the year I had numerous assignment savers. When I told my parents what I had been doing, they bought me a book on ventriloquism and a monkey puppet. That's how I began. It's very convenient to be able to speak without moving your lips—especially when you have something to say, but you don't want anyone to know that you were speaking.

Lip Position

You'll need a mirror while reading this section of the book. It doesn't have to be large. A hand-held mirror is fine.

Now look at yourself and smile. Go ahead. Give yourself a big smile and try to look happy. Say "Cheese."

Some people show their teeth when they smile. Others don't, but you will notice that every ventriloquist while performing smiles with his mouth open. There's a very important reason for this.

Some people suppose that ventriloquists speak with their mouths closed. This is untrue. No one can talk with his mouth closed.

Instead, the ventriloquist adopts a comfortable *lip position*. A lip position is a smile that shows your teeth, but leaves room between your lips through which to talk. It must be comfortable and not too tight. Your lips should be loose. The tighter they are the more unnatural it will look and the more your lip movement will be noticed. A good lip position is comfortable, convenient and looks natural.

The best way for you to discover your lip position is to look in the mirror and smile naturally with your mouth open. Now breathe through your mouth. Is there room? Now gently blow air out of your mouth, trying to hold your lips still.

Remember, a good lip position is firm but not tight. It shouldn't look like a fake grin. Relax. Be natural.

Look in the mirror. Find a good lip position, leaving room between your lips through which to talk. Is it comfortable? Does it look natural? Good. Now, using your lip position, say "Hi."

Did your lips move? Try it again. You didn't need your lips to say "Hi," did you? Yet you probably wanted to use them. Why? Not because you needed them, but because you've always used your lips to talk.

With the Puppet

From this point forth, whenever you talk using your lip position, speak with a puppet's voice. As was explained in the previous chapter, this voice should be distinctly different from yours. As a beginner, simply raise it or lower it. I find that my lips move less with a slightly higher voice than with a lower one or than with even my own normal voice.

Look in the mirror and say "Hi" with a puppet's voice. This voice, or a variation of it, will develop as you practice, and it may soon become the voice of a partner who will know you as well as you know yourself.

If you already have a puppet at this point, let him mouth the words whenever you speak using your lip position. If you don't have a puppet, use your hand or even create a puppet out of a sock. Begin searching for a "friend" with which you can practice.

My first "friend" was a gray sock puppet whose eyes kept falling off. Of course I never used him in public, but he was there during many of those first practice sessions. My next puppet was a monkey, Herman, which I used widely for nearly six years. Even now, on occasion, he'll come out of retirement and perform again.

The voice that will develop out of your new lip position is not just a voice without a source. Practice it as if your partner were speaking the words. This will also help you to develop good, coordinated mouth movement with your puppet.

Now take your puppet, look in the mirror and say "Hi" in his voice.

Good job. If your lips moved some, that's all right. They're used to moving when you talk, and it's a hard habit to break.

How old are you? Well, that's how long your lips have been moving. Don't expect them to be still overnight. The more you practice, the less they will move. The more you practice, the better you'll become. That's the big rule to ventriloquism: practice, practice, practice.

The Alphabet

Let's begin with the alphabet. Look in the mirror with your puppet and try to say each letter. As you do, try to distinguish which letters require lip movement. (Here's a hint: there are only six of them.)

a b c d e f g h i j k l m n o p q r s t u v w x y z

On which ones did you *have* to use your lips?

That's right. It's impossible to say a "b," "f," "m," "p," "v" or "w" without using your lips. Before dealing with these "difficult" letters, however, let's first practice the letters you *can* say. Look into the mirror and try the following list:

a c d e g h i j k l n o q r s t u x y z

Did your lips move much? The more you practice, the less they'll move. As a beginner, practice this section ten to fifteen minutes every day. Before long your lips won't move at all.

You can also use your finger to help train your lips not to move. Pretend that you are telling someone to be quiet. Where do you put your finger? Now smile with your lip position and press gently with your index finger. Use your index finger to help your lips stay in the correct position while you speak. Try the above list again and continue to practice the list before moving further.

Now try to say these words:

> *cat, light, kitty, ugly, dog, darkness, state, skate, hand, nice, run, car, ring, song, dance, cute, shingle, English, concern, clean, crazy, rose, store, house*

Practice these phrases:

> *He hurt his hand.*
> *Diane didn't do diddlie.*
> *Ring around a rosy.*
> *Sue sent Sally to the store.*
> *Ted tickled the toy.*
> *See Jane run.*
> *There goes the kitty-cat.*
> *I saw you there.*
> *Sheila said she likes this state.*
> *Could I ask a question concerning cars?*
> *Do you know the answer?*
> *I like to sing and dance.*
> *This is great!*

Congratulations! You are well on your way to becoming a ventriloquist, but remember to continue practicing the above exercises daily.

So how are you doing so far? Well? Yes? That's wonderful, but don't get too excited. Be sure that you always understand what each chapter is explaining before you venture ahead.

4. Speaking without Lip Movement

The alphabet contains six letters that are impossible to say without using the lips. These are "b," "f," "m," "p," "v" and "w."

"So how," you ask, "does a ventriloquist pronounce them?"

Good question. The answer is easy: he doesn't. Your puppet will never say a "b," "f," "m," "p," "v" or "w." Instead, these letters will be replaced by other letters *which sound like them* but which can be spoken without lip movement.

For instance, rather than saying "b," you will say "d." For "f" you will say "th" as in "*th*ink." For "m" you will substitute either an "n" or an "ng" sound as in the word "ki*ng*." For "p" you will use "k" or "t." For "v" you will substitute a "th" sound as in "fa*th*er." Finally, for "w" you will pronounce an "ooooo" or an "l" sound.

Pronouncing the difficult letters is a matter of substitution. It's an ability that will become both easy and natural as you practice. If sometime you have to say "The fat basketball player finished the match," you'll *naturally* say "The that dasketdall tlayer thinished the ngatch."

The Letter "B"

The letter "d" is the substitute for the letter "b." Thus, rather than saying "bee," you'll say "*d*ee." Rather than saying "bus," you'll say "*d*us." Rather than saying "boat," you'll say "*d*oat."

Practice this substitution with the following words and phrases:

buckle, bat, sideburn, big, celebrity, battle, bed, bread, board, bakery, brand, abandon, belt, cabinet, bubble, baboon, bug

The big, bad baboons beat the celebrities at basketball.
Unbuckle your belt if you abandon the boat.
I broke the brand-new cabinet during the battle.

The Letter "F"

The "th" sound in the word "*th*ink" is substituted for the letter "f." Thus, rather than saying "father," you'll say "*th*ather."

Rather than saying "fly," you'll say "*th*ly." Rather than saying "flat," you'll say "*th*lat."

Practice with the following words and phrases:

friend, sheriff, final, official, fool, coffee, after, fickle, Frank, safety, float, life, fearful, thirty-four

Life is safe if one doesn't follow a fool.
Your friend the sheriff finally found the official file.
You could fall after drinking fifty cans of coffee.

Try a mixture of substitutions:

baffle, fabulous, buffoon, bountiful, beautiful

Before you fly to the benefit, be sure to find the flight tickets.
By finding Frank safely, the sheriff showed his fabulous ability.

The Letter "M"

The letter "n" or the "ng" sound in the word "ki*ng*" is substituted for the letter "m." Thus, rather than saying "mother," you'll say "*n*other" or "*ng*other." Rather than saying "match," you'll say "*n*atch" or "*ng*atch." Rather than saying "mixture," you'll say either "*n*ixture" or "*ng*ixture."

Practice with the following words and phrases:

men, might, smile, game, minute, mammoth, time, multimedia, myself, transmission, monster, commissioner, something, mommy

Many mumbling mice are making midnight music in the moonlight.
The mighty men tamed the monstrous mammoth.
Something small might remind you concerning a mixture of matters.

Try a mixture of substitutions:

mumbling, family, famous, fumble, muffled, mob

My mother's transmission began to make many different sounds.
Being mindful of the man's dilemma, the commissioner began to smile.

Famous men begin to mumble, trying to answer many different matters.

The Letter "P"

The letters "t" or "k" are substituted for the letter "p." It is best to choose one or the other all the time instead of trying to use them both interchangeably. Thus, rather than saying "picture," you'll say either "*t*icture" or "*k*icture." Rather than saying "puddle," you'll say either "*t*uddle" or "*k*uddle." Rather than saying "printer," you'll say either "*t*rinter" or "*k*rinter."

Practice with the following words and phrases:

> *pillow, plot, happy, pickle, deputy, power, suspect, pizza, prayer, separate, pudding, pepper, punch*

> *Pucker power is a preposterous practice.*
> *The Pied Piper played a pitch that peeled the paint.*
> *The proud deputy punched the suspect that escaped the prison.*

Try a mixture of substitutions:

> *pitiful, pumpkin, map, powerful, pompous*

> *Peter always makes important plans to pepper his pizza.*
> *Because my hamburger had pickles, I felt pain in my stomach.*
> *The opinion of the Pied Piper was a powerful pressure on Capitol Hill.*

The Letter "V"

The "th" sound in the word "fa*th*er" is substituted for the letter "v." Thus, rather than saying "victory," you'll say "*th*ictory." Rather than saying "value," you'll say "*th*alue." Rather than saying "victim," you'll say "*th*ictim."

Practice with the following words and phrases:

> *victory, vanish, vine, river, receive, divorce, discover, individual, severe, nervous, evening, vanquish, live, video, vulture*

> *The divorcee vowed to live victoriously.*
> *Evening vanishes to receive the night.*
> *Vincent discovered the vanishing video.*

Try a mixture of substitutions:

ventriloquism, fervent, five, vent figure, overboard, prevention, develop, forever, volumes, vampire

The main key to ventriloquism is practice, practice, practice.
The vent figure vowed to make people laugh at the ventriloquist.
The vampire vanished after fighting the victorious individual.

The Letter "W"

The sound "ooooooo" or the "lu," "l" sound, is used as the substitute for the letter "w." Thus, rather than saying "want," you'll say "*ooo*-ant" or "*l*-ant." Rather than saying "with," you'll say "*ooo*-ith" or "*l*-ith." Rather than saying "water," you'll say "*ooo*-ater" or "*l*-ater." "W" is the easiest of the "difficult letters" for which you need to substitute.

Practice the following words and phrases:

what, when, where, wood, want, war, wagon, wicked, with, worm (Note: Did you notice the "m" in worm? When you said it, did you remember to use a substitute for it?)

The worm wiggled when he wanted it to waggle.
Would you want worms when you could eat waffles?
We went to war with wooden warriors.

Try a mixture of substitutions:

wisdom, wolf, waver, whipping, swamp, swim, beware, waffle

What did you want when you were whispering to me?
The bumblebee wouldn't have stung him if he hadn't swung at it.
The wounded warrior found a soft place to sleep that evening.

Now try the following phrases:

I'm going to be the best ventriloquist in the world.
I like to practice.
I love this book.
"Hey, buddy, why aren't your lips moving?"

The Disguise

At first the substitutions may seem very unnatural. They probably sound odd to you. This raises a question: if they sound odd to you, then why don't they sound odd to an audience? In other words, "Why didn't I ever notice a ventriloquist substituting letters?"

The reason that letter substitution is not obvious when listening to a professional ventriloquist is that the substitutions are disguised. As you continue to practice these sections, you will need to begin disguising them as well.

The key is to hide the substitutions. This is accomplished by emphasizing, or stressing, the part of the word away from the difficult letter.

For instance, if you were going to say "bananas," you would stress the latter part of the word. Rather than saying "Ba-nanas," you would say "baNANAS." Rather than saying "Victory," you would say "vICTORY." Rather than saying "submission," you would say "submISSION." Rather than "Bus," it's "bUS."

Now read the above four paragraphs aloud using your lip position, making substitutions for the difficult letters and practicing this "stressing" effect. Try to read them aloud without moving your lips.

Review

Now that you know the secret of speaking without lip movement, you are well on your way to becoming a professional ventriloquist. But just knowing the secret won't make you improve. You must practice. The rule to becoming better is to practice, practice, practice.

Return to this chapter often. Practice the exercises daily, and before long these substitutions will become completely natural. You won't even have to think about them.

5. Ventriloquist Dialogues

Welcome to chapter 5. You're doing great, but it's time to take a test. Try to answer the following questions:

1. What are the three basic keys to the illusion of ventriloquism? (See chapter 2)
2. What is a lip position? (See chapter 3)
3. Which six letters of the alphabet require lip movement and need substitutions? (See chapter 3)
4. What letters do you substitute for the "difficult letters?" (See chapter 4)
5. How do you disguise ventriloquial substitutions? (See chapter 4)

How did you do? If you struggled over any of these questions, review those sections of the previous chapters before continuing the book. Remember, you're not reading this book to get to the last page. Instead, you're studying it to become the best ventriloquist possible. Here's another question: how do you become the best ventriloquist possible? The answer: practice, practice, practice.

Continue to practice the alphabet ten to fifteen minutes a day, and keep reviewing the exercises in chapters 3 and 4. They are your foundation, and you'll only be as good as your foundation allows.

If you're now confident in the basics, then you're ready for the remainder of this chapter. Slip on your puppet and enjoy the following scripts. Keep your partner alive, practice the difficult lines in front of a mirror and let the substitutions become second nature. Have fun, and remember, your puppet likes to laugh. He's human too, you know!

School
(approximately 5 minutes)

VENTRILOQUIST: Hi, I'm (*your name*), and this is my friend (*figure's name*).

FIGURE: Hello there.

V: So how are you doing, (*figure's name*)?

F: Well, I'm not doing so well.

V: What's wrong?

F: Well, you see, I've got this mean teacher at school.

V: A mean teacher?

F: That's right. Come to think of it, she looks like a saint.

V: A saint?

F: Yeah, Saint Bernard! Actually, she's got teeth like stars.

V: Teeth like stars. Because they're shiny and bright?

F: No. Because they come out at night! And she's got real attractive eyes.

V: Attractive eyes?

F: They keep looking at each other! And she's got a wart right on the end of her nose.

V: A wart?

F: It's really not that bad. Her upper lip covers it!

V: Now, (*figure's name*), I've never seen your teacher, but she can't be that bad.

F: Oh, she is! Like the other day, we were sitting in class and we were learning to make paper airplanes.

V: In class?

F: Right.

V: The teacher was teaching you to make paper airplanes?

F: No. Johnny was. Well, anyway, I had this great, big, beautiful one. And I got back, and I threw it. (*Rears back and swings forward as if he is acting out the throwing motions*) And it soared, and it glided, (*Leans to the far right and left and around in the air as he is talking, as if he is watching the plane sore and glide*) and it flew, straight into . . . (*Pauses, looking both ways, and then loudly, as if shocked*) THE TEACHER'S HAIR!

V: The teacher's hair!

F: So she turned around and the whole class started laughing, and she said, "Order, I want order here!" So I stood up and said, "Give me a hot dog, extra mustard, hold the relish!"

V: You didn't.

F: I did.

V: Did she get mad?

F: Oh, she got really mad, and she said, "(*figure's name*), go to the office." So I got up out of my chair—slow, real slow. And I started walking towards that door—slow, real slow. And I walked out that door—slow, real, real slow. (*Acts very dra-*

matic, as if telling a grand story) And suddenly there she was!

V: Who?

F: One of my girlfriends.

V: *One* of your girlfriends?

F: That's right.

V: How many do you have?

F: Three.

V: You have three girlfriends?!

F: That's right. (*Looks into the air as if daydreaming*) Mary, Beth, (*Pauses*) and Lassie.

V: Lassie?! (*figure's name*), Lassie's a dog!

F: You ought to see the other two! Anyway, I walked into the office and sat down, and she sat down next to me. So I leaned over—slow, real, *real* slow, and I . . . Well, I . . . I kissed her!

V: Right there?!

F: That's right.

V: In the office?

F: That's right.

V: Did the principal see you?

F: That's right!

V: What did he do?

F: He came over to me, and he said, "Son, I'll teach you to kiss a girl in school." And I said, "You don't have to, sir, I already know how!"

V: Oh no.

F: So he grabbed me by the shirt collar, and he started shaking me and shaking me. And he said, "Son, I think the Devil's got a hold on you." And I said, 'I do too, sir, so why don't you let go?"

V: You're kidding.

F: Plus, I think he's blind.

V: What do you mean?

F: Three times in the office he asked me where my hat was, and it was on my head the whole time.

V: Well, (*figure's name*), say good-bye and we'll talk about school later.

F: Okay. Good-bye.

V: Good-bye.

Math
(approximately 5 minutes)

VENTRILOQUIST: Hi, I'm *(your name)*, and this is my friend *(figure's name)*.

FIGURE: Hello there.

V: So, *(figure's name)*, how do you like school?

F: Closed!

V: Don't you like going to school?

F: Actually, I don't mind the going, and I don't mind the coming. It's the staying that bothers me!

V: Well, what do you like in school?

F: Girls.

V: Surely there's something else.

F: Yeah. I'm kinda fond of lunch and recess too. I even like bathroom breaks.

V: No. I mean, what subjects do you like?

F: None.

V: *(figure's name)*, I don't like to hear that.

F: Then don't listen!

V: I mean, I don't like to see you like this.

F: Then invest in blindfolds.

V: Well, what do you take in school?

F: Anything not glued down.

V: How are your grades?

F: They're all under water.

V: Under water?

F: Yeah. They're all below *sea* level.

V: What do have in English?

F: A good nap.

V: What do you have in Spelling?

F: A great time!

V: How come?

F: Sally sits across from me.

V: I mean, what grades do you have?

F: "Ds."

V: What about math?

F *(Whispers)*: An "F."

V *(Loudly)*: An "F"!

F: Well, tell the whole world!

V: How come you have an "F" in math?

F: It's all your fault.

V: My fault? What did I do?

F: If you hadn't taught me all those magic card tricks I would have gotten an "A."

V: What do magic card tricks have to do with this?

F: You see, my teacher asked me to count from one to twenty.

V: What did you say?

F: I said, "One . . . two . . . three . . . four . . . five . . . six . . . uh . . . seven . . . (*Pauses*) . . . eight . . . uh . . . (*Pauses*) . . . nine . . . (*Pauses*) . . . ten, jack, queen, king!"

V: Jack, queen, king!

F: Yeah.

V: Well, I think I can help you with your math.

F: You can?

V: I think I can. I'll ask you a few simple questions and you just answer them the best you can. Okay?

F: Okay.

V: Let's say that you take a piece of paper and tear it in half. What do you have?

F: Trash.

V: I mean, do you have fourths, halves . . .

F: Halves!

V: That's right. Great. Now let's say that you tear those in half. What do you have?

F: Fourths.

V: Great. Then you tear those in half.

F: Eighths.

V: Great. Then you tear those in half. Now what do you have?

F: Confetti!

V: Let me ask you another question.

F: Okay.

V: Let's say you have ten dollars in one pocket and five dollars in the other. What do you have?

F (*Pauses, looking at his pockets, and then, surprised*): Someone else's pants!

V: I don't think this is going to work.

F: Ask me one more question.

V: All right. Let's say your uncle makes four hundred dollars a week.

F (*Surprised*): He does?

V: He does. And he gave you half.

F (*Excited*): He did?

V: He did. Now what do you have?

F: Heart failure!

V: This isn't going to work.

F: Well, why don't you let me ask you the questions?

V: Ask me questions? Sure. Go ahead.

F: What is one plus one?

V: Two.

F: Correct. What is two plus two?

V: Four.

F: Correct. What is four plus four?

V: Eight.

F: Correct. What is eight plus sixteen times two divided by ten plus one hundred and thirty-eight?

V: What do think I am, nuts?

F: Correct again!

V: (*figure's name*), I'll help you with your math later. Say good-bye to the people.

F: See you later.

V: Thank you and good-bye.

Singing/Dirty, Rotten Liar
(*approximately 4 minutes*)

VENTRILOQUIST: Hi, I'm (*your name*), and this is my friend (*figure's name*).

FIGURE: Hello there. Hey, you know what?

V: What?

F: I want to sing a song!

V: That's a great idea. Can I sing with you?

F: Oh no. Remember what happened the last time we sang together?

V: The last time?

F: Yeah. The *last* time!

V: Not really.

F: Do you remember that real high note?

V: High note?

F: Yeah, that real high one.

V: Uh . . . Oh, you mean that *real* high note.

F: That's the one.

V: I hit that note.

F: You didn't hit it. You *smashed* it.

V: Now, (*figure's name*), singers happen to run in my family.

F: Well, they certainly should after that!

V: I don't think you understand. You see, I sing from the heart.

F (*To audience*): If he had a heart he wouldn't sing!

V: Well, I just sing to kill time.

F: You definitely kill something!

V (*Dreamily*): But when I sing, you should hear the people clap . . .

F (*Quickly*): . . . their hands over their ears! (*Laughs*)

V: So you don't want me to sing?

F: Don't get me wrong. I love for you to sing solo.

V: You love for me to sing solo?!

F: Sure. *So low* I can't hear you. Plus, I don't think you know the words.

V: That's kind of hard to believe. I seem to have *a hand* in everything you do.

F: You see, I wrote this song.

V: *You* wrote a song!

F: Yeah.

V: Well, let's hear it.

F: All right. Here goes. (*Clears throat*) Here goes. (*Clears throat*) Here goes. (*Clears throat; then, to the audience*) Excuse me for a moment. (*Clears throat a few more times and then makes a grotesque noise and spits*) Now I'm ready.

V: Go ahead and sing.

F: All right. (*The figure sings a song that everyone knows and one that is appropriate for the occasion: e.g., "She'll Be Coming Around the Mountain," "The Brady Bunch," "Jingle Bells," etc.*)

V: (*figure's name*), you did *not* write that song.

F (*Shocked*): How did you know?

V: I've heard that song many times before, and so has everyone else!

F (*To audience*): You have?

V: Yes, they have.

F: Uh oh! I'm so ashamed. (*Tries to hide by tucking his head into the ventriloquist's chest, or if it is a wooden figure he can turn his head backward*)

V: (*figure's name*), you should have known better than to tell a lie.

F: Don't call it that. 'Cause if there's one thing that I just can not stand, it is a dirty, rotten LIAR!!!

V: What about you?

F: Well, that's different.

V: No, it's not different. (*figure's name*), a lie is a lie.

F: But it was just a little white lie.

V: (*figure's name*), there's no such thing as a little white lie. You should always tell the truth, because if you don't, then people will never know when to believe you.

(Different endings can be added at this point depending on the audience. Are you performing in a school, at a church, for a benefit, etc.? You may also want to include more jokes at the end.)

Miscellaneous Dialogue
(approximately 5 minutes)

VENTRILOQUIST: Hi, I'm (*your name*), and this is my friend (*figure's name*).

FIGURE: Howdy.

V: You know, (*figure's name*), I want to start out tonight with a bang!

F: Great! Let's shoot you.

V: I mean, I want to start with something snappy.

F: A rubber band?

V: Something catchy.

F: A mouse trap?

V (*Not paying any attention to the figure's comments*): I know! Why don't you introduce us today?

F: Me!

V: Sure.

F: All right. Here goes . . . Ladies and . . . Uh . . . Uh. . .

V: Gentlemen.

F: Gentlemen. Yes. Thank you . . . Today I would like to introduce to you the world's greatest ventrikolist . . .

V (*Correcting the figure*): Ventriloquist.

F: Hey, who's doing this introduction?!

V: Go ahead.

F (*Clears throat as if to begin again*): Today I would like to introduce to you the world's greatest ventrikolist . . .

(*The ventriloquist begins to smile*)

F: . . . the best ventrikolist that has ever ventriloquated in the history of ventriliqual history . . .

(*The ventriloquist is really enjoying this*)

F: . . . the greatest ventrikolist that ever walked on the face of the earth. I would *like* to introduce him to you, but unfortunately *he* couldn't be here tonight.

V: (*figure's name*), I don't think you understand. (*Whispering to figure*) I want you to make me sound really well known. Okay?

F: All right . . . Uh . . . (*Turning to audience*) I would like to introduce you to a great ventriloquist. Everyone knows his name. Here he is, that great ventriloquist . . . (*Loudly to ventriloquist*) What did you say your name was again?

V: Never mind. So how are you doing today, (*figure's name*)?

F: I'm doing great!

V: How come?

F (*Proudly*): Because I bought a dog today.

V: Bought a dog? How much did it cost?

F: He cost ten thousand dollars.

V (*Impressed*): He must be a pretty special dog.

F: Oh, he is. He's part bull.

V (*Pauses*): Part bull?

F: Yeah.

V: Which part?

F: The part about the ten thousand dollars!

V: You know, I like dogs.

F: I know you do. I saw your last girlfriend.

V: She wasn't *that* bad. (*Dreamily, as if remembering*) She had the complexion of a peach.

F: Yeah, yellow and fuzzy

V: She really wasn't *that* bad.

F: Oh yeah. I've seen better heads on a nail.

(*The ventriloquist is silent*)

F: But I loved her fur coat.

V: I never bought her a fur coat.

F: You didn't have to. It was growing out of her skin!

V: What about *your* girlfriend?

F: She's wonderful. In fact, she threw a flower at me today.

V: That's sweet.

F: And it hurt too!

V: How can a flower hurt?

F: She didn't take it out of the vase.

V: Well, (*figure's name*), why don't you say good-bye?

F: No, I ain't goin'.

V: You *ain't* going?

F: That's right. I ain't going.

V: (*figure's name*), watch your grammar.

F (*Surprised*): Where is she?!

V: Who?

F: My grandma.

V: I didn't say your grandma.

F (*Still looking at the audience*): Nope. My grandma *ain't* here.

V: No! Not grandma. Ain't! Ain't!

F: You know, you really should watch your grammar.

V: That's what I said. It's incorrect to say "I ain't going." It's: "I *am* not going"; "you *are* not going"; "he *is* not going."

F: Well, *ain't* nobody goin'?

V: Let me explain. You see, "I" is a pronoun.

F: *You* is a what?

V: Forget it.

F: I already did.

V: You know, I would really like to explain this to you before we go.

F: Okay.

V: Now why is it incorrect to say "I ain't going?"

F: Because you ain't gone yet.

V: Say good-bye, (*figure's name*).

F: Good-bye (*figure's name*).

V: That's not what I meant.

F: Don't look at me. YOU said it!

V: I suppose I did have a *hand* in it.

F: That's right. Good night everyone.

V: Good-bye.

The Telephone
(approximately 5 minutes)

VENTRILOQUIST: Hello everyone.

FIGURE (*Staring at the ventriloquist*): Wow! Is that your nose or are you eating a banana?

V: (*figure's name*), watch your mouth!

F: I can't. My nose is in the way.

V: You know, I brought something really special out here tonight. (*Holds up a small piece of paper*)

F: What is it? My paycheck?

V: No. *You* work for free.

F (*To audience*): I think that's called slavery!

V: It's a phone number. Somebody wants to talk to us. It must be really important.

F: Great. Let's call him.

V: That's a good idea. (*Places paper next to the phone, picks up the receiver, and begins dialing the number*) Hello? Hello?

PHONE VOICE: Hello? Hello?

F: Wow! It's an echo.

V: Hello?

PV: Hello there. How are you doing?

V: Fine.

F: Can I talk to him? Please let me talk to him. Please.

V: Okay. (*To phone*) Would you like to speak to (*figure's name*)?

PV (*The following lines should be spoken quickly*): To who?

V: To (*figure's name*).

PV: To who?

V: To (*figure's name*).

PV: Is he there?

V: He's here.

F: I'm here.

V: That's right.

F: Yeah. Sure.

PV: Okay. Put him on.

V: He'll talk to you.

F: Great. (*The ventriloquist holds phone to figure's ear*) Uh . . . Howdy.

PV: Hello there. Is this (*figure's name*)?

F: That's right.

PV: So tell me, what are you going to get that ventriloquist for his birthday?

F (*To ventriloquist*): He wants to know what I'm going to get you for your birthday.

V: I'd like to know too.

F: You would?

V: Sure.

F: Okay. Close your eyes.

V: All right.

F: Are they closed *real* tight?

V: They're closed real tight.

F: Now what do you see?

V (*Pauses*): Nothing.

F: Well, that's what you're getting.

V: That's almost as good as the gift you gave me last year.

F: What did I get you last year?

V: You gave me a nice pair of banana peels.

F: They were slippers.

(*The ventriloquist chuckles*)

F: I almost gave you a gift that keeps on giving.

V: What? Jewelry?

F: No, a pregnant rabbit.

(*The ventriloquist is silent*)

F: Hey, do you know what I want for *my* birthday?

V: I'm scared to ask.

F: I want a skunk!

V: A skunk?

F: Yeah, a great big one with a huge white stripe down its back.

V: Where are you going to keep it?

F: In your room.

V: My room?

F: Sure.

V: What about the smell?

F: He'll get used to it.

V: (*figure's name*), don't you know how to keep a skunk from smelling?

F: Sure. Cut off its nose.

V: No. Just don't buy one, and *no*, I am not going to get you a skunk for your birthday.

F: In that case, I'll just take a card.

V: Would you like a serious card or a funny card?

F: No, a credit card!

PV: Hello? Hello? Are you still there?

F: Yeah. I'm still here.

PV (*Angrily*): Where did you go? I've been waiting on the phone for a long time.

V: That *was* rude of us. (*To vent figure*) Why don't you tell him you're sorry?

F: Do I have to?

V: Yes you have to. Now tell him you're sorry.

F: Hello?

PV: Yes?

F: You're sorry!

V: (*figure's name*)!

PV: Oh yeah? Well, I'd say that you're pretty close to a dummy!

F (*Glances at ventriloquist*): I'd say that you're probably right. (*Turns to phone*) What's that? I didn't quite hear you. (*The phone voice can no longer be heard, but the figure looks surprised and excited*) You don't say! (*Continues looking even more excited*) You *don't* say! YOU *DON'T* SAY! (*To ventriloquist*) You can hang up now.

V: What did he want?

F (*Pauses*): He didn't say.

V: Why don't you say good-bye?

F: See you later.

V: Have a great evening.

6. Line Delivery

The delivery of a line determines the difference between a good, a fair and a lousy performance. If the audience has to strain to understand you, how can you be effective? They should be able to sit back and enjoy the performance.

Imagine a contest in which all the ventriloquists performed the same dialogue. What would distinguish the winner? How could you determine the best one? Line delivery would be the deciding factor. It's the fine touch that distinguishes between who is good and who is the best.

Line delivery is much more than just speaking clearly. It concerns three specific areas:

1. Emphasis
2. Speed
3. Gestures

Emphasis

People are emotional, and our emotions determine how we emphasize our words. Your partner is not emotional—he's a dummy who has no emotions, so you must put emphasis on his phrases according to how he is supposed to feel.

Surprise. Shock. Mirth. Anger. Happiness. Sadness. Sarcasm. You instill all of these feelings by emphasizing the words in different ways.

In real life our feelings determine this emphasis, but ventriloquism is not real life. It's acting, a scenario. So rather than having the feelings controlling the phrases, the phrases must express the feelings. Your emphasis must tell the audience what is going through your mind. How do you feel? How does your partner feel?

Don't just repeat a memorized script. How dull and boring! Instead, *feel* the dialogue. *Experience* the emotion of the scene. Then let your words do all the talking.

Just as a door swings on a hinge, the emotion, or tone, of a sentence swings on the hinge of the voice inflection. Voice inflection refers to the change in tone or loudness that stresses a particular word or phrase in a sentence. By emphasizing a particular word you can change both the sentence's mood and its meaning. For example, repeat the following sentence, emphasizing the italicized word in each of its variations:

"You shouldn't have done that."

1. Anger: "You *shouldn't* have done that!"
2. Sarcasm: "You shouldn't have done *that.*"
3. Humor: "*You* shouldn't have done that."

Do you hear how the emphasis sets the tone? Obviously the stressing of certain words can change and even distort the meaning of a sentence. Be careful not to destroy a good joke by using the wrong emphasis.

Practice using emphasis and developing different emotions by experimenting with the following sentence:

"You ate my cake."

Say it with:

1. Anger
2. Sadness
3. Shock

Did it sound something like:

1. Anger: "You *ate* my cake!"
2. Sadness: "You ate *my* cake."
3. Shock: "*You* ate my cake!"

Speed

For someone who is unaccustomed to public speaking, there is a temptation to be like Superman, going faster than a speeding bullet. Many people, when they stand before a crowd, open their mouths and the words pour out at incredible speeds. Like horses at the starting gate, once it opens, they're gone. Then, with a pant at the end and a wipe of the brow, they're finished. They said all the proper words, but they spoke so quickly that no one enjoyed the performance.

While performing your act, be careful not to talk *too* fast. "Fast talkers" may make some profit, but not as ventriloquists. Slow down. Remember, you're having a conversation.

Set a steady pace for the dialogue. How fast do you normally talk? That's a good speed, and it's natural for you.

Also, use shifts in speed to avoid a monotonous tone. Be careful not to get stuck in a rhythm so constant that it compares to the dripping of water torture. One way to avoid this is to occasionally implement a rapid yes-I-did, no-you-didn't type conversation.

Here's an example:

FIGURE: I want to sing a song.
VENTRILOQUIST: They don't want to hear you sing a song.
F: Yes, they do.
V: No, they don't.
F: Yes, they do.
V: *No, they don't.*
F: But . . .

Or:

F: He did?
V: He did.
F: Wow!
V: That's right.
F: He did.
V: Indeed.

Here's an example from a ventriloquist telephone dialogue using three voices at a rapid pace:

VENTRILOQUIST (*To telephone*): Hello?
PHONE VOICE: Hello.
V: Hello?
PV: May I speak to (*figure's name*)?
V: To whom?
PV: To (*figure's name*).
V: To whom?
PV: To (*figure's name*).

FIGURE: I'm here.
V (*To telephone*): He's here.
F: That's right.
V: Indeed.

Gestures

In the same way that voice inflection can add vocal emphasis, gestures add visual emphasis. Gestures are actions of enthusiasm that control the quality of your performance. They add professionalism and are effective in setting the tone. In addition, they are not limited to the ventriloquist. Even the vent figure can make gestures.

Two types of gestures will be addressed here:

1. Hand Gestures
2. Facial Gestures

1. Hand Gestures

While performing and practicing, free your arms. Let them move. Don't allow nervous tension to stick them to your side, and keep your hands out of your pockets. Pocketing one's hands is a common response to being in front of an audience. Many people don't even realize that they do it. As a ventriloquist, your free hand should remain out of your pocket, except for those brief moments when it becomes an appropriate gesture.

As you speak, let your hands move freely and naturally. Become observant of how you commonly use your hands in everyday, normal conversation. Then implement those gestures into your routine. If they don't come naturally as you perform, then plan them and practice them. If you have not practiced them, when you stand before an audience your hand may seek a hiding place, becoming frozen to your side or stuck in your pocket.

Stand in front of the mirror and, as you practice, attach the proper hand motions to the proper sentences. Work on timing. Avoid unnatural movements. If it doesn't feel right, it probably isn't.

Let the gestures complement your words. For instance,

don't say "You . . ." while talking to your partner and point to yourself instead.

Gestures back up your words and add extra meaning. They draw an emotional picture. If you are supposed to be angry at your vent figure, which is more natural? To put your hand on your hip, or to put your hand in your pocket?

The natural response is to put your hand on your hip. Such an action can paint a picture of aggression: you and your partner are in conflict. Picture in your mind an angry mother scolding her child. Where are her hands? In her pockets? No. They're on her hips. She's mad, and that's a natural gesture.

But although gestures can enhance your words, be careful not to overuse them. As with many other aspects of ventriloquism, use them, but don't abuse them. Overuse of anything can distract the audience from your performance.

Your partner can also use hand gestures. You can attach a rod to one of his hands, by means of which you can operate his arm: it is best to use the arm that is closest to you. At first the audience will notice the rod, but as the puppet becomes real to them, they will only pay attention to the hand gestures. This can be a very effective way of making your partner spring to life.

Make the hand gestures realistic. Practice them and, again, be careful not to abuse them.

2. Facial Gestures

The wink of an eye. The raise of an eyebrow. The drop of a jaw. These are a few of the many facial gestures that can enhance your performance. Even as you become mindful of and practice hand gestures, you must also devote time to practicing facial gestures. The right glance to the audience at the right moment can make or break a joke.

To create the illusion of making the puppet actually look alive, you must give him human mannerisms as well. These include facial expressions. Yet facial expressions are very difficult for your partner: in a sense he's handicapped in this way. He can't raise his eyebrows (at least, most can't). Most vent figures can't wink. They can drop their jaws, but they can't wrinkle their foreheads. They're fairly limited in this area, which makes the expressions that they can do even more meaningful and important. From them develops much of the figure's personality.

A key to giving your partner realistic facial expressions comes by watching the head movements of the people around you every day. Put yourself in your figure's place. If you were to express yourself by moving just your head, your mouth and perhaps your eyes, how would you do it? A cocked head can represent a number of situations. A dropped mouth can represent surprise. A drooping head can show sadness or disappointment.

Let's examine how a figure could respond in certain situations:

Surprise: The vent figure's mouth quickly opens as wide as possible and his head jerks forward. His mouth remains open, and he looks at the audience with quick head and eye movements.

If this reaction occurs while he is already looking toward the audience, his first movement should be to look at you before turning to glance at the people. The head movement should follow the movement of the eyes, maintaining the same speed.

Thought: The vent figure should move his head slowly and directly, cocking it either to the right or to the left. His eyes, likewise, should move diagonally upward, looking toward the ceiling and off into space.

Embarrassment: When you're embarrassed, how do you feel? How do you act? Do you look people straight in the eyes? Probably not. When you feel about the size of a mouse, you usually want to hide. When the figure feels embarrassed, he too should exhibit these tendencies. For instance, if you are using a hand puppet, have him duck his head into your chest. After all, he wants to hide too.

If you're using a wooden figure who can't duck his head into your chest, have him look away from you. Or better yet, have him turn his head in an 180 degree spin, completely away from the audience. Although this breaks the rule of making the figure look human (since neither you nor I can spin our heads all the way around), it can be very humorous if done correctly.

Shame: Since being embarrassed is similar to being ashamed, many of the same actions are useful, although there are some differences. Let's say, for example, that your figure has just told you that a whale swallowed him while he was fishing last Saturday. He tells an elaborate story of his traumatic experience, but he makes a big mistake and his lie becomes known. Although he wants to hide, he probably would not duck his head into *your* chest. After all, you're the one who is confronting him with his falsehood. If he is a hand puppet, you could have him sink in his seat, look at the ground and slowly shake his head as if he realizes that what he has done is wrong. If he is wooden and can't sink in his seat, have him close his eyes (if possible) while he looks toward the ground and shakes his head.

Excitement: When your partner is excited he should speak faster than normal. His movements should be quick and rapid. You may even want to have him jump up and down in his seat.

Your figure can mimic any emotion. Put yourself in his shoes (although they're probably too small for you). How would you feel? How would your gestures—your hand movements, your head movements and your facial expressions—portray this mood? Your vent figure should exhibit the same reactions.

Remember that your vent figure should be alive from the moment he leaves his carrying-case to the moment he returns there—even when nobody is watching. Everything he does should portray human actions and human qualities. This is an essential part of the ventriloquist's illusion. The more alive the figure looks, the better you have become as a ventriloquist and the more your audience will enjoy your performance.

7. Special Effects

In the previous chapter you learned that the more human your vent figure appears, the better the illusion will be. In this chapter you will discover how to create other lifelike effects that will greatly enhance your performance. You will also learn how to perform what an audience might consider to be some of the harder illusions of the ventriloquist.

In this chapter you will learn how to produce the following effects:

1. Sneezing
2. Blowing the nose
3. Clearing the throat
4. The distant voice
5. The muffled voice
6. The echo effect

Sneezing

You can write an entire dialogue around your partner having a cold, but to perform such a routine you must perfect some extra human effects. For example, attempt to allow your puppet to talk as if he is having severe sinus problems. (This "muffled" sound is similar to the muffled voice that you will learn later in this chapter.) Then let your figure sneeze periodically throughout the script.

To teach your figure to sneeze, you should pay attention to how you yourself sneeze. It begins with an irritation. You take several deep breaths. Then the sneeze comes with a variety of sounds. Your puppet can do the same—without requiring lip movement.

After a couple of sneezes you might have your figure begin to sneeze again. He takes a few deep breaths . . . but it seems to go away. Then, as you begin to talk again, he suddenly sneezes on *you*, burying his nose deep into your shirt sleeve.

By being creative with this special effect, you can add an extra edge to your performance skills. Everyone enjoys a sneezing figure, for it adds variety and a bit of humor to the dialogue.

Blowing the Nose

Having the figure blow his nose is my favorite special effect. Of course making him blow his nose doesn't mean that you have to blow yours. All the sounds for this special effect are done in the throat. Practice making noises that sound like the one you want to create. For instance, what does it sound like when you blow your nose? Listen to the sound. Then attempt to create that same sound or a similar sound in your throat. The weirder the noise the better. Even if it doesn't quite sound normal, who said that your partner was normal? The audience will be able to distinguish what you are doing because hopefully you (or perhaps even a volunteer from the audience) are holding a handkerchief to his face.

To use the "blowing the nose" sound effect, you can implement a mini-dialogue in the middle of your script. The dialogue might go something like this:

FIGURE (*Interrupting the ventriloquist*): Do you have a handkerchief?

VENTRILOQUIST: I think so. (*Begins searching his pockets*)

F: Hurry! I need a handkerchief. Hurry!

V (*Searching faster*): I'm looking! (*The situation is becoming frantic: suddenly the ventriloquist pulls a handkerchief out of his pocket and brings it to the figure's nose just in time. The figure can either sneeze or just blow his nose*)

F (*After a prolonged blow*): Thanks. I feel better.

(*The ventriloquist looks at the handkerchief, holding it with only two fingers as if he is afraid to touch it. He drops it on the ground a few feet from him*)

At this point the dialogue resumes, but a few moments later it happens again . . .

F: Do you still have that handkerchief?

(*The ventriloquist looks at the ground and realizes that he can't reach it*)

F: Hurry! I need that handkerchief.

V: Uh, could I get someone to help me? Could you please

help me, sir? (*Chooses someone near by who has been enjoying the performance*) Could you bring me that handkerchief? Be careful: you don't know where it's been.
(*The whole time the figure has been begging and pleading for the handkerchief. If the volunteer is slow in getting the handkerchief, the figure should blow his nose on the ventriloquist's shirt sleeve.*)
F: Thanks. I feel better.

Clearing the Throat

Making your figure clear his throat is easy. You simply clear your throat very loudly. Overexaggerate the sound. Then, as an added feature, you might even have your figure pretend to spit on the ground.

The conversation might proceed like this:

FIGURE: Can I sing a song?
VENTRILOQUIST: Sure. Go ahead.
F: Okay. (*Clears his throat several times and then turns to the audience*) Excuse me for a moment. This won't take long. (*Continues to clear his throat and then finally pretends to spit on the ground*)
V: (*figure's name*), don't spit.
F (*If it's a wooden figure*): It's only sawdust.
   (*If it's an animal puppet*): It's only a hair ball.
   (*Or even*): It's only last night's supper. Wow, look at that green bean!
V: Why were you clearing your throat anyway?
F: Good singers always clear their throats before they sing.
V: Are you a good singer?
F: No, I just had to clear my throat!

As you continue to practice, these special effects will develop over time. Whenever you have a few spare moments . . . whenever you're in your living room with nothing else to do . . . whenever you're driving to work, smile using your lip position and begin experimenting with them. (You may want to wait until you're alone to do this. Otherwise, people might think that you're odd. Next you might even start *talking to yourself*!)

The Distant Voice

The distant voice is how your figure's voice or another voice sounds when it is far away from you. With such an illusion you are trying to make it appear that the voice is coming from backstage, from down in a cellar or from some great distance. You can also use it as the voice of a flea in a flea circus.

To present this appearance, practice the following:

1. Raise the voice an octave: it should be a higher-pitched voice than normal
2. Produce the voice at the back of your throat: this should naturally tighten your throat muscles and help you with the raised voice
3. Prolong the vowel sounds of the words that end the sentence: for instance, rather than saying "Hello. Who are you?", have the figure say "Hello-o-o. Who are yo-o-ou?"
4. Make the voice appear to be talking at full volume, although the volume that you are hearing is low. When you project your voice loudly, you give a different emphasis to words than when you are engaged in a normal conversation. In order to obtain this emphasis, take the words that you are going to say with your distant voice and pretend that you are saying them from the bottom of a deep well. You want the person at the top to hear what you are saying.

Use the following sentence to practice:

"Help! Get me out of here!"

If you were shouting this from the bottom of a well, how would it sound? It would probably be something like, "He-e-elp! Get me out of he-e-e-ere." With the distant voice you do the same, except you raise it a pitch higher, produce it from the back of your throat and make it sound soft, as if it is being said loudly from a distance.

Now practice this distant voice effect as it is being used in the following dialogue about an invisible hole (be sure to always practice with your puppet):

DISTANT VOICE: Hello!
VENTRILOQUIST: Hey, who's down there? (*Looking at the ground*)
FIGURE: Where?
V: There.
F: Where?
V: There.
DV: Here. Hey, are you that ventrilokolist?
V: Ventriloquist.
F: Yeah. A guy who talks to himself.
DV: So, is (*figure's name*) up there?
V: He sure is.
F: Howdy.
DV: (*figure's name*), can you lend me thirty dollars?
F: I'm sorry. I can't hear you.
DV (*Louder*): Can you lend me thirty dollars?!
F (*Louder*): I can't hear you!
DV (*Almost yelling*): Can you lend me thirty dollars!?!
F (*Yelling*): I still can't hear you!!!
V: (*figure's name*), I can hear him!
F: Then *you* lend him thirty dollars.

The Muffled Voice

The muffled voice sound effect makes the figure's voice appear to come from within an object. For example, let's say that you walk on stage without your puppet. You begin to explain to the audience that you can't find your partner. You're worried and concerned, but suddenly you hear a noise coming from a nearby suitcase on the floor.

"Did you hear that?" you ask the audience. "It sounded like (*figure's name*)." (*You bend down so you can hear better . . .*)

Let's stop there for a moment. Have you ever heard someone talking from inside a closed compartment? Hopefully you've never heard anyone talking from the inside of a suitcase or a car trunk, but if you have, you know that the voice

sounds muffled. In other words, it's not clear. It sounds like
a person trying to talk with his mouth full of rocks or mar-
bles. It is still quite loud, only muddled. This is the muffled
voice.

The muffled voice is an effective tool that can be used in a
variety of ways. You can talk to your partner inside a suitcase or
an invisible ant inside a soda can. And if you perfect it enough,
you can always make the little man inside the ketchup bottle
talk during dinner.

The following steps will help you to develop a muffled voice,
but this effect, like the others, comes only through practice
and hard work:

1. Take a deep breath: you're going to need a lot of air
   for this one
2. Curl your tongue into the bottom of your mouth below your teeth-line, and hold it in this position as you
   speak: this will give the voice a nasal tone and will
   hinder its clarity
3. Slightly tighten your throat muscles and produce the
   voice from the back of your throat

As you are developing the muffled voice, you will notice
that the words are not always distinguishable. When the figure
says "Help! Get me out of this," it may sound like "Elp! Et ne
ou a dis." Such is the muffled voice, and since you want your
audience to understand what the voice is saying, you should
repeat his lines after him.

Practice (with your figure, of course) the following dialogue
continuing the situation presented earlier:

(*You bend down so you can hear better . . .*)
V: (*figure's name*), is that you?
F (*Muffled*): Help! Get me out of this!
V: Get you out of this? How did you get in it?
F (*Muffled*): You see, I was running across this stage because
   I was trying to stop a fight between two guys, and I fell in.
   (*While the figure is talking, the ventriloquist raises the lid. He is
   facing the audience and he opens the lid towards the audience so*

that they can not see the lifeless puppet inside. As he raises the lid the
figure's words gradually become unmuffled and his normal voice
returns)
V: Now let me get this straight. You were running across this
   stage because you were trying to stop a fight between two
   guys.
F: That's right.
V: So why were you running?
F: Because I was one of the two guys.

The Echo Effect

One of the most impressive special effects in ventriloquism
is the echo. In this section you are going to learn to make the
figure's voice echo his words as he speaks them.

Imagine the announcer of a boxing match. He says "ladies,"
and the word echoes throughout the arena, "and gentlemen,"
and these words echo as well.

An echo is the result of sound bouncing back and forth between objects or walls. With each bounce it becomes softer
and softer until it can no longer be heard. Such is the echo
effect.

Have your partner repeat the following line, using the same
volume for each word:

Ladies, ladies, ladies, ladies, ladies

Now picture the boxing announcer. At the top of his lungs
he said "LADIES!" Pretending that you are him, use the same
emphasis and energy in projecting the first "ladies." Then
with each "ladies" following, let the volume get gradually
softer until it is hardly a whisper.

Repeat the following line:

LADIES, ladies, ladies, ladies

The next step in the echo effect, if the word begins with
a consonant, is to omit the first consonantal sound of every
word following the first one.

In the alphabet every letter is a consonant except for "a," "e," "i," "o" and "u": these are called vowels. In the echo effect, "y" is also going to be considered a vowel.

Hence, since the word "ladies" begins with a consonant, the consonant will be omitted after the initial pronouncement.

For example, practice the following line with the beginning consonants omitted:

LADIES-adies-adies-adies

Now connect all the words together as one single unit. Give each word the same emphasis, but let the last consonant cover up the first consonant of the next word, unless it begins with a vowel. There shouldn't be a pause between the words. They should all run together as in the following example:

LADIESadiesadiesadies

Overall, to develop a realistic echo effect you must

1. Take a deep breath
2. Strongly project the first word
3. Let each "bounce" of the word become softer than the last
4. Let each "bounce" of the word have the same emphasis as the first one
5. Omit the first consonant sound in each echo if the word begins with a consonant
6. Let the words run together as they bounce back and forth, softer and softer, and try to pronounce them as if they were one big, long word
7. Let the figure's lips (or your lips as the case may be) move only on the first pronouncement. Remember, the rest is the echo and no one's lips move when listening to an echo

Using these rules, echo the word "ladies" again.

Good. Now try the word "and." Remember that you omit the first consonantal sound in each echo if the word begins with a consonant: the word "and" begins with a vowel, not a consonant, and therefore this rule won't apply.

Echo the word "and" by pronouncing the following:

ANDandandand

Now try "gentlemen."

GENTLEMENentlemenentlemenentlemen

A final rule that was not mentioned above concerns long words such as "gentlemen." Both the word "ladies" and the word "and" have less than three syllables, but "gentlemen" is a three-syllable word. In other words, it is composed of three parts with a main vowel sound: gen / tle / men. Whenever you come across a three-syllable word that you desire to echo, a good rule of thumb is to affix the beginning consonant of the middle division, in this case "t," to the beginning of the last echo.
 Hence:

GENTLEMENentlemenentlemententlemen

Notice that the last echo is not "entlemen" but "tentlemen." This effect is caused because each syllable in an echo echoes back and they overlap with one another. By the end of the echo, since the word is so long, the middle syllable is echoing at the same time as the first syllable. The duplication of the middle consonant is an indication of that overlap.
 With one- and two-syllable words, this rule is unnecessary. The echo doesn't last long enough for them to overlap. It applies only to three- or more syllable words.

Now attempt the entire introduction:

LADIESadiesadiesadies
ANDandandand
GENTLEMENentlemenentlemententlemen

Congratulations! You've just echoed your first introduction, and the more you practice, the better it will sound. Again let's review the rules of creating an echo:

1. Take a deep breath
2. Strongly project the first word
3. Let each bounce of the word become softer
4. Let each bounce of the word have the same emphasis as the first one
5. Omit the first consonant sound in each echo if the word begins with a consonant
6. Let the words run together as they bounce back and forth, softer and softer, and try to pronounce them as if they were one big, long word
7. Let the figure's lips (or your lips as the case may be) move only on the first pronouncement (remember, the rest is the echo, and no one's lips move when listening to an echo)
8. If the word has three or more syllables, attach the beginning consonant of the middle division (e.g., the "t" in the case of gen / tle / men) onto the beginning of the last echo. This signifies the overlapping of the echoing syllables

Now, using your puppet, practice the following dialogue:

VENTRILOQUIST: Hi, I'm (*your name*), and this is my good friend (*figure's name*).
FIGURE: Wait a minute! Wait a minute! How come you always get to do the introductions?
V: I don't know. I always figured it was part of my job.
F: Can I do it tonight?
V: Sure.
F (*Echoes*): Ladies . . . and . . . gentlemen . . .
V (*Looking around in dismay*): Where did that echo come from?
F: From your hollow head!

Welcome to the wonderful world of special effects. By now you know how to make your figure sneeze, blow his nose, clear his throat, make a distant voice, make a muffled voice and develop an echo. None of these extra effects are essen-

tial, although they are fun to implement and audiences enjoy
them. Nor do they come naturally. These effects are perfected
through hours of practice. If you struggled with any or all
of them in this chapter, don't be discouraged. Be patient.
Continue to practice and they will develop in time.

8. Scriptwriting

Scriptwriting can be easy if you follow three simple rules:

1. Keep a joke file
2. Use proper script organization
3. Consider the type of program for which it is being written

The Joke File

A joke file is an index of all the jokes you have told or that you might tell in the future. Whenever you find a new, good joke, add it to your file. Before long you'll have your own resource for scriptwriting.

Of course, organization is important in keeping a joke file (a small container of 3"×5" or 4"×6" note cards should be sufficient for the task). After all, the jokes won't do you any good if you can't find them when you need them. This is a joke file, not a disorganized trash heap of jokes written on anything and everything and all thrown into the same area of your room or office.

You can organize the file in numerous ways. Listed below are two of the most efficient methods.

The first lists the entire joke on an index card. The card is labeled and filed according to its subject and topic headings. For example:

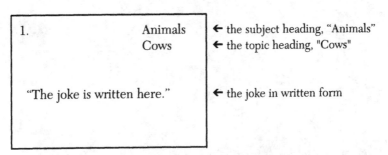

The second method does not contain the actual jokes, but is a catalog of them. It's like the card catalog in a library, because each card tells you where to find jokes on certain subjects. This method allows you to list hundreds of jokes from joke books, etc., on a relatively small number of cards. For instance:

```
┌─────────────────────────────────┐
│                  Animals    ← the subject heading
│  1. Cow      J #1 /p. 7
│  2. Skunk    J #2 /p. 24
│  3. Cat      J #6 /p. 35
│  4. Dog      J #2 /p. 12
│  5. Dog      J #4 /p. 21
│  6. Moose    J #3 /p. 2
│                                 │
└─────────────────────────────────┘
```

This card is a reference card. It tells where to find jokes on certain subjects. For example, the subject of the card above is "Animals." If you wanted to tell some jokes about animals at a farmer's convention, you might turn to this card.

Then you would look at the joke titles or names. You can also pencil in a brief description or key phrase for each joke, to remind you which one it is.

For instance, if you wanted to tell a joke about a skunk, you would look under the subject "Animals." You would then look for the title "Skunk." Once you found the right title, you'd know where to look. For the card above, you would look on page 24 in Joke Book #2 (J #2). This method is quick and easy, and now you're ready to tell a joke about skunks that *really stinks.*

These are two efficient methods of organization, but don't limit yourself to them. Find one that works for you. You might even try combining the two for quicker and easier access. In cases such as these, practicality is far more important than technicality. Usefulness is the key. However you choose to organize your joke file, make sure that it is user-friendly and not too complex. Organization is great so long as it doesn't get in the way and hinder its own purpose.

Script Organization

There are two major ways to organize a script:

1. The Joke Format
2. The Message Format

1. The Joke Format

The joke format applies to scripts that contain only jokes. These dialogues are pure entertainment and have no purpose beyond making people laugh. In them the ventriloquist is not trying to convey a specific message: he just wants the people to have a good time and to enjoy themselves.

To follow this format, organize the jokes according to four simple rules:

1. Begin the script with your second-funniest joke
2. End the script with your funniest joke
3. Counter a good joke with a bad joke
4. Organize the jokes according to theme

Always begin your script with the second-funniest joke, for "you never get a second chance to make a good first impression." The first joke will set the tone for the remainder of the program. It prepares the audience for what is yet to come, so you want it to be good.

The last joke should be the funniest of all. A good ventriloquist will always leave the audience wanting more. Leave them laughing. Let their last memory be the best by saving the best for last.

Counter the best jokes with the worst jokes. This system avoids dry spells within a routine that can leave the audience bored. If a joke flies over your listeners' heads, it's all right because a better one is on the way.

Remember that no one likes to be left hanging. Every joke you tell should be like a paragraph—it should be tied to the one before it so that the routine as a whole flows together. I have heard dialogues that were jagged and constantly hopped from one subject to another. Although all the jokes were good, they didn't connect. The entire routine just didn't have a rhythm to it: it was like each member of a band trying to play a different song at the same time.

A realistic ventriloquist script is a humorous conversation, and normal conversations do not change subjects every five seconds. If you choose to write a script by throwing together a group of unrelated jokes, you may lose your audience's attention. Although such a script may be humorous and although it may be good, it will not be as effective as it could be. It's all right to change the subject two or three times, but try to limit the shifts and try to tie all the loose ends together.

For example, let's say you have some excellent jokes about cows and some excellent jokes about being hungry. When you make the shift from one subject to the other, organize a smooth transition. For example, as a transition from "cow" jokes to "hungry" jokes, you might say:

FIGURE: All this talk about cows has make me hungry.

Or as a transition from "hungry" jokes to "cow" jokes:

FIGURE: I'm hungry for a hamburger. You know, that reminds me of my uncle's cow . . .

Or you could even say:

VENTRILOQUIST: Well, maybe if we change the subject, you'll forget you're hungry.
FIGURE: Okay.
V: What do you want to talk about?
F: How about cows?
V: Okay. What about cows?
F: Well, you see, my uncle . . .

Transitions are easy to develop. Be creative with them, and let them be the threads that bind your script together. Have fun with them, but make them realistic. Make them smooth. Even make them humorous.

2. The Message Format
Unlike joke-formatted scripts, message-formatted scripts attempt to convey a particular point. Your reason for standing before an audience might be greater than just trying to entertain people or to make them laugh: you want to teach them something, or you're bringing them a message.

For instance, in a school you might be trying to stress the idea "Say no to drugs," or "Don't drink and drive." Whatever the message, let the jokes become the dish in which the pie is served. The message is the pie: that's the reason you are there. The jokes are the dish that carries the message and makes it a delight to the audience.

To me, ventriloquism is much more than entertainment. Even if I can make an audience laugh for five minutes, when I am gone, so is the laughter. But if I can use humor to teach people something, when I leave they will hopefully be better because I was there. My purpose for being there may be simple or it may be serious, but I always try to leave the audience with some sort of message.

There are two primary ways to organize such a presentation:

Method A
> I. Introduction
> II. Second funniest joke
> III. The main body of jokes
> IV. The theme
> V. The funniest joke

Method B
> I. Introduction
> II. The funniest joke
> III. The other jokes
> IV. The theme

Use Method A when you are presenting a light-hearted or simplistic message. Begin with an introduction. For example:

VENTRILOQUIST: Hi. I'm (*your name*), and this is my friend (*figure's name*).
FIGURE: Howdy!

Now they know who you are, and they also know who your friend is. Introductions are always good places to begin, even if an emcee has already introduced you.

I used to be very stiff and formal with my introductions. I would say, "Hello. My name is . . ." Then I realized that whenever you introduce yourself in normal conversation, you usually don't say "My name is . . .": instead you're more likely to say "I'm . . ." I therefore switched from the formal to the casual to create an appearance of everyday conversation.

Under Method A, the remainder of the dialogue is the same as the joke format with the difference that your message comes before the final joke. It's also all right to have several jokes following the theme, but don't overdo it. It's better to be too brief and leave them wanting more, than to run too long and beat a dead horse.

The only difference in Method B is that it does not end on a humorous note. This order is for more serious themes when you want to leave the audience with the message fresh in their minds. For deep topics such as these, additional jokes might distract them from the real reason you are there.

No matter which method you use, if you are teaching a lesson you should give your partner the most important lines. No offense, but both children and adults listen more to what "the dummy" says than to what you say. His words are more likely to stay with them. Ventriloquism can be an excellent teaching tool, especially for children, so don't be afraid to use your talent to better the world around you.

Consider the Type of Program

1. The Audience

Before you write a script, consider for whom you are writing it. Will you be delivering it to children or adults? Is it a banquet setting or an outdoor festival? Will the audience be seated or will they be coming and going, with people constantly walking past? Will you have their full attention or will they be eating while you perform? Is there a theme to the show?

All of these factors play a role in how you will wish to present yourself. Be especially mindful of who will be in attendance. I once was performing at the opening of a new hamburger restaurant, and I told a joke that praised McDonald's. Big mistake: McDonald's was one of their competitors, and the owner didn't appreciate my comment. His exact words were

"Hang that boy!" The situation was very embarrassing. I had used poor judgment.

2. Length

Dialogue lengths vary considerably. Talent competitions usually limit the length of a program to three minutes. If you are an opening act, five to seven minutes is common. There are even times when you *are* the show. Three minutes is the shortest program I ever did. One hour is the longest.

The typical show is between fifteen and twenty-five minutes. In other words, you'll need more than one dialogue. In a twenty-five minute program, I would recommend performing three or four different skits, perhaps with several different characters. This means leaving and reentering the stage several times.

If you plan to leave the stage during the show, be sure that you have already prepared everything backstage. The audience will begin to get restless if you leave for more than about thirty seconds. Another suggestion is to let the audience hear you call your figure while you are leaving the stage: "Hey, Andy, where are you?"

You may even have him answer, "I'm over here!"

If you have planned to perform two dialogues back-to-back with the same figure, I recommend leaving the stage between the two. Remember, during a show you don't always *have* to be doing ventriloquism. Add variety. For example, after the first segment of a lengthy program, you may want to come out without your partner and briefly tell the audience a little about yourself. Don't try to be a comedian, just let them get to know you. This will add a little variety to the show, so that you're not always coming and going and performing a routine in between. Nevertheless, don't get so carried away talking about yourself that the audience can't wait to see the "other" dummy.

Another idea for variety in lengthy programs is to lead the audience in a song. Come back onstage without your partner and simply tell them that you want to teach them a song. This is especially good for children and youths. Kids usually can't sit still for long. I recommend having them stand up and sing a fun song with hand motions, then telling them that you are going to bring out your partner again and that you'll be right back.

"But wait," someone might say. "If I lead a 'wild and crazy' song, how do I settle the kids down again?"

Don't worry about it. The kids will settle themselves down. In situations such as this it's all right if the kids get a little energetic, because they'll calm down the moment you begin your dialogue. They *want* to hear the script, and kids will listen to a ventriloquist (actually, to the vent figure) more than they will listen to almost anyone else. They will hush themselves to hear you.

9. Memorizing the Script

By the time the performance day arrives, you should have your script written, memorized and thoroughly practiced. Remember the key to ventriloquism: practice, practice, practice. In other words, by the time the performance day arrives you should be well prepared and comfortable with your presentation. Procrastination and ventriloquism do not go hand in hand.

The previous chapter dealt with scriptwriting. You don't have to write your own scripts, of course: you can buy them. You can not, however, pay someone else to memorize them for you.

"Oh no," you may be thinking. "I have the worst memory in the world."

That's all right. Most people don't consider themselves to have a good memory. Some might say they have no memory at all, and half of them are right. But the only reason that memorizing seems so difficult is because we, as a society, never do it.

Be careful. Here is a snare you may face: when you stare at a three-page script that you know you need to memorize, there is a lurking temptation to dread the task. Indeed, it may seem like a huge task, but truly most of the hardship is in your mind.

I used to despise memorizing new scripts, but the more I did it, the more I realized how quick and easy it can be. Memorization does not have to be difficult, and the more you memorize, the easier it becomes. In time you will probably even develop a pattern, a certain system that works well for you.

For example, whenever some people memorize, they read the item over and over and over again, until they can finally recite it. To me, that's not memorization: that's torture. They have their styles, however, and I have mine. Listed below are a few possible methods that you might find useful. Experiment with them to see which works best for you.

Memorization by Familiarity

Begin by reading through the script. Don't concern yourself with the specifics. Seek to get the gist of it. Become famil-

54

iar with the order and the basic pattern. Develop a mental outline of the routine. At this point you may not be able to recite a single line of it, but that's all right. Ventriloquist routines are not a series of one-liners randomly compiled together, but a well-ordered series of jokes. As you learn the jokes, you'll naturally learn the lines. Likewise, as you become familiar with the ins and outs of the script, you'll find that you are memorizing it while avoiding much of the drudgery of memorization.

Memorization by Section

As with the above method, this system encourages memorization by using an outline. Outline your script on paper. Name the jokes to help you remember them.

Your outlined dialogue might look something like this:

    I. Introduction
   II. Joke #1—I'm Hungry
  III. Joke #2—Kitchen Joke
   IV. Joke #3—Spinach and Broccoli
    V. Joke #4—Cows
       Etc . . .

Rather than attempting to memorize the whole routine at one sitting, memorize the individual sections. Memorize the first joke and practice it with your vent figure. Once you're comfortable with it, memorize the second joke and practice it alongside the first joke. Then the third . . . and the fourth . . ., etc. Work your way through the entire script, and before long you'll be practicing the whole dialogue in its proper order.

Memorization Line by Line

As with the previous system, in which the script was learned section by section, this method involves memorization line by line. In other words, you learn the first line before moving to the second. When you can repeat the first and second lines, you move to the third. When you can repeat the first, second and third lines, you begin on the fourth. You continue this way until the whole script is committed to memory. It's like learning to walk—you take it one step at a time.

Look at the first line. Read it. Close your eyes and try to repeat it. Picture the words in your mind. What are they saying? Repeat the line again and keep repeating it until you feel comfortable with it.

Say it fast. Say it slow. Give it proper emphasis. Focus all your attention on each word. Find a place that is quiet where you won't be distracted, so that you can maintain your concentration. Then, before continuing to the next line, start to recite again, beginning with the first line and working forward from there.

This is called "backtracking," because you constantly step backward before moving forward. Each time you have memorized another line, you return to the very beginning and then repeat the script in its entirety, or at least to the line that you last memorized. You review before continuing.

This is a time-consuming process, but by the time you're finished you'll know the script from front to back. You'll be able to quote it in your sleep.

When memorizing, always be patient; in order to retain the script, you must review the script. That means: practice, practice, practice.

Memorization is necessary for ventriloquism, but it doesn't have to be torture. Allow yourself plenty of time to memorize the script. (In other words, don't wait until the night before your performance.) Constantly review. Take plenty of breaks. Try to approach the dialogue from a fresh perspective each time you work on it.

10. Practicing the Script

Football teams don't go to the Super Bowl without many hours of practice. Athletes don't win the gold without training. Plays aren't performed without previous rehearsal. And good ventriloquists don't walk on stage without learning their acts. As with all skills, practice perfects ventriloquism and will make you the best at it that you can be. Athletes don't win the contest on the day of the game: the game was won beforehand in the practices that have prepared them. Even a diamond would remain dull if the rough edges weren't cut away.

For the ventriloquist, practice is of paramount importance. How well you do onstage will be determined by how well you do in practice. Devoted trainees for the Olympics practice daily. Military boot camps drill the soldiers with daily routines. The health-conscious person knows that exercise doesn't help unless you do it dedicatedly three to five times a week. The art of ventriloquism similarly requires a consistent practice schedule.

As a beginner, this is the most critical time for you. As you read this book you are building a foundation, and a house is only as good as the foundation on which it is built. If the foundation is bad, the house is bad. If your practice habits are bad now, they will remain bad. Now is the time to develop an unvarying routine of practice.

In the future the amount you practice will depend on how prepared you feel. Some days you may practice for two hours. Other days you may practice for fifteen minutes, and, yes, there will be days when you won't practice at all. For now, however, you should practice for at least thirty minutes a day, at least three to five days a week.

Review the lip exercises. Begin writing and memorizing scripts. Continue to develop your partner's personality. Use your time wisely.

Thirty minutes may seem like a lot, but it's really not. You might spend at least that much time watching television, and many ventriloquism performances are between fifteen and twenty minutes, so you'll need to prepare something that long at the very least.

At the beginning your voice may become tired after only fifteen minutes. If this is the case, don't push yourself. Never strain your voice in practice. Practice for fifteen minutes and then let your voice rest for an hour. Then practice for another fifteen minutes. It's better to begin refreshed several times than to push yourself through one long practice, hurting your voice.

In time your vocal cords will adjust to the strain of speaking in a different pitch. When I am out of practice, my voice can only last about twenty minutes before becoming stressed, but at my best it becomes strained only after about an hour. The more you practice, the more your throat will become accustomed to producing your partner's voice.

Once you have commited your script to memory, concentrate on your appearance. As you practice, station yourself in front of a mirror. Always practice in front of a mirror so that you can see from the audience's point of view.

The first time through the script, concentrate on yourself. How are you delivering your lines? Where are you looking? When do you look at the vent figure and when should you look at the audience? Are your lips moving? How does it sound? Are the nonpronounceable letters being de-emphasized or are they obvious?

If there are problematic sections or sentences, devote the most time to them. Practice is not for the purpose of memorizing, but for the purpose of producing a better appearance. What can you do to make the dialogue more realistic? How can you make it better? Be creative. Be inventive. I've used echo effects to enhance certain facets of the dialogue, and once I even taught my vent figure how to whistle slightly.

Another good habit to build during practice is exaggerated lip movement.

"Exaggerated lip movement? I thought my lips weren't supposed to move."

That's right. They're not supposed to move—at least, not when your puppet is talking—but when *you* are speaking it's a different matter. One good way to cover up slight lip movement when your figure is talking is to exaggerate your own lip movement. Of course, don't overdo it. Don't overexaggerate, but speak clearly and distinctly. Enunciate all your words properly.

After concentrating on yourself, concentrate on your partner. How do his lines sound? Are his lips moving along with the right words? When does he look at the audience? When should he look at you? Does he look alive, and how could you make him act more realistically?

Now shift your focus to the routine in general. How does it sound as a whole? Are you pleased? Displeased? Why? And what areas need more attention? Practice hand and facial gestures, and begin to experiment with tone, speed and emphasis (see *Line Delivery*, chapter 6).

Once you're fairly confident, perform the dialogue in front of friends or family members. Ask them to critique you, and be prepared: they'll probably tell you the truth, which may not be what you want to hear. When people critique you, they usually don't point out all the things you do right. Just remember that a critique is constructive criticism. It's constructive, not destructive. In other words, it is criticism that helps rather than hurts.

Your critics are evaluating you to help you become better. Take their advice. Examine it and weigh it to find what you need to change, to find the areas to which you need to devote more practice.

Don't get mad at them for being honest with you. The wise person will take criticism to heart and will become better for it. Only a fool scoffs at correction.

Finally, while practicing, always imagine yourself doing your best. Picture yourself as the best of the best, doing the best that you've ever done. If you picture yourself making mistakes, when the time comes you'll probably find a way to make them.

It's extremely important to always imagine yourself succeeding. Say to yourself, "They will love my performance, and I will enjoy giving the gift of laughter." Always picture yourself being the best that you can be.

You must build your confidence, and your confidence is built through practice, practice and more practice. The more you practice now, the less reason you'll have to be nervous later.

Keep a positive attitude, and if anything ever goes wrong during a show, keep your head held high. Remember, you're the best ventriloquist in the room. Of course, you're probably the *only* ventriloquist in the room . . .

11. Props

Besides your partner, there are two major props that you will need to consider:

1. The vent stand
2. The vent carrying-case

The Vent Stand

As you prepare your dialogue, you'll need to decide whether you will stand, sit or hold your vent figure on your knee.

Some ventriloquists like to perform while sitting, but I prefer to stand. In ventriloquism, voice projection (or diaphragm speaking) is very important, and sitting can affect this ability. When you whisper, you talk quietly; when you project your voice, the volume is loud enough to carry to the farthest seat in the room. You are speaking as if you are talking to the person on the back row. You're not shouting, however: you are pushing the air out with your diaphragm, a muscle located below your lungs. Sitting can thus make projection more difficult. This is one reason that I prefer to stand.

On occasion I will sit while performing, but these are rare instances. Let us suppose, for example, that you are going to present a program to a group of children who are seated on the floor. If you stand, you will tower over them. Children always relate well when you are on their level. In instances such as these, although I prefer not to sit, the advantages outweigh the disadvantages.

Yet despite my preference, standing presents a problem. If you stand, where is your puppet going to sit? He can't just dangle in midair. After all, he's human too (or so he says).

You have two options. You can use a footstool on which you will place your foot to allow the vent figure to sit on your knee, or you can use a vent stand. The vent stand is your partner's seat during the performance. It can be purchased or easily made.

To make one, you need a good-looking piece of stained

wood, a microphone stand and a microphone flange adapter. The adapter will have three screw holes, and it will thread onto a standard 5/8″ microphone stand. Simply use three screws to secure the adapter to the center of the wood. (The wood piece, which will become the seat for your vent figure, should be approximately 11″×13″ and at least 1″ thick.) Then screw the thread of the adapter onto your microphone stand. You've just created a seat for your partner. You may also want to place some velvet on the top of the board, where your elbow will be resting. Some people even attach a fringe or cover the stand with bright-colored material. Be creative, but make it look professional.

The advantage of using a microphone stand is that you will be able to adjust its height. Puppets and vent figures come in a variety of sizes, but with this stand, one size fits all. Before you practice or perform, adjust the stand so that your vent figure is a little shorter than you are. You don't want to be eye to eye with him. After all, *you're* the ventriloquist.

The Vent Carrying-Case

The vent carrying-case is your partner's home away from home. I call it his bedroom, but no matter what term you choose, you will need one. The vent carrying-case is the bag in which you will transport your figure. It doesn't have to be elaborate, and most people will never see it. The key to choosing the right bag is convenience. You want it to be large enough to carry your partner without wrinkling his clothes, but it should not be too bulky. If your figure is a professional wooden figure you'll also want to pad the inside to protect him from damage. Otherwise padding is unnecessary. Customize both the bag's fit and its size to suit your needs.

You may also want to stock the carrying-case with "emergency" supplies. For example, I carry a hair brush and a comb. Incidentally, these are not for me, but for my puppet. (He likes to look good too!) You may also want to carry a pen, some paper, any tapes that you may need, business cards and perhaps even some safety pins in case your partner has a last-minute clothes-fitting problem. Preparation always pays in the end.

12. The Audience

Friend or Foe

The members of the audience aren't your enemies. They're your friends. If you like them, they'll like you. Don't perform *for* them, however, and don't perform to impress them. Perform for your own enjoyment. When they sense that you're having a good time, they'll have a good time as well.

Once I was scheduled to do a forty-five minute program. I walked out on stage as normal. I had poise and a big smile—a great first impression. But as I began my routine, something just wasn't right. A few of the youths were talking among themselves. Very few were laughing. This isn't always the ventriloquist's fault. Every audience is different. Some are in a good mood, others are in a bad mood, but these kids were completely out of it. They were hardly catching a single joke.

I thought to myself, "This is torture. Forty-five minutes of being in front of a dead crowd. Why don't I just cut it short and get it over with?"

Then another thought occurred to me. "Wait a minute. They're a captive audience. They're not going anywhere, so who cares what they think? I'm here. I enjoy performing, so I will just enjoy myself. I'm going to have a good time and get paid for doing it."

What happened? I enjoyed myself, and by enjoying myself, I gave them my best. By the end of the evening they were laughing at every joke. What began as a bad audience transformed into a good one. In fact, they were one of the best that I've ever had.

The audience can tell whether you are enjoying yourself. If you have fun, they'll have fun. If you're bored, they'll be bored. If you laugh and have a great time, they'll laugh and have a great time.

Your attitude sets the tone, so be positive and be energetic. This is one key to being successful. Your enthusiasm and enjoyment greatly affect your audience. From the moment you walk on stage, you should have your head held up. Be poised. Walk with confidence. Look them in the eyes.

Rather than repeating a set of prepared jokes or a routine as though you've practiced it a hundred times, let it be fresh and alive. Although you may have heard it so much that you can repeat it in your sleep, this is the first time that the viewers have heard it. Don't rob them of its freshness. If you're tired of the dialogue, they'll sense it, and it will affect their response. Will they laugh? Or will they sit there as bored as you?

After the Show

Most people are not observant. If they were to watch the ventriloquist closely, they would notice that his throat moves as he pronounces the words. This movement is unavoidable, and trying to hide it by wearing high-collared shirts or turtleneck sweaters only makes it more obvious. Some people may notice your throat's movement, but very few will ever mention it.

Yet in every crowd there's *that* person—you know the one. He wants you to know how smart he is by letting you know that he saw your throat move. He may even tell you that he saw your lips move, but, of course, he'll follow this comment with, "But you're still a really good ventriloquist."

When someone mentions that he saw your lips move, just nod your head and smile. Don't get upset. Don't let it ruin your night. Just put it behind you.

Then there are those other people—the ones who think you're talking with your mouth closed and are somehow, perhaps, speaking through your nose. These people are the least observant, but probably the most amazed (and amusing).

When you see them after a performance, they may ask you to "say something with your mouth closed," or to "throw your voice and make Joe talk." Of course *you* know that both of these requests are impossible. They don't. They are mystified by your talent, so don't ruin their amazement by attempting something you can't do. Save yourself by saying something like this:

"I'm very sorry, but I only perform when my vent figure is with me."

This is a polite letdown that pulls you out of a situation that would reveal the secret of ventriloquism.

You may also meet some children who will beg you and beg you and beg you to get your puppet out for them. They want to see him again. Or, worse yet, they want to play with him. Be kind to them. They have pure intentions, but explain to them that your puppet is asleep and you don't want to wake him. He's had a long day.

Finally, after a show you will probably have people telling you how much they enjoyed what you did. Shake their hands firmly. Give them a big smile and just say "Thank you."

Be professional and courteous from the moment you drive into the parking lot to the moment you drive out again. And remember, always smile. This says a lot about a person.

13. Publicity

"Now that I'm a ventriloquist, how do I schedule performances? How do people find out about me?"

First, ask yourself, where do I want to perform? Do you want to perform in schools, churches, hospitals, etc.? Why did you become a ventriloquist? Surely when you read about performing you pictured yourself in a certain setting. What setting did you see yourself in? Were you sharing your act with children at a day-care center? With the mentally disabled? Were you at an amusement park?

Where you desire to perform will direct you to the kind of publicity you need. For example, if you want to volunteer to perform for children in a hospital, you may simply want to call the hospital staff and see if they are interested. Never be afraid to take the initiative. If they say no, it's their loss. You can always find some other place to volunteer.

The extent to which you want to perform will also determine how much publicity you need. If you only desire to perform once in a blue moon, you probably don't want massive publicity. On the other hand, if you want to be scheduled somewhere every week, strong publicity is essential.

The means of public exposure are as numerous as the stars in the sky. Nevertheless, this chapter will examine five common ways of becoming known. Not all of these may apply to you, but they are broad enough that just about anyone can use them. They are as follows:

1. The information source
2. Fliers
3. Talent shows and community events
4. Talent agencies
5. Word of mouth
6. The follow-up letter

The Information Source

Every day you are surrounded with innumerable information sources: the daily newspaper; the topical magazine; the

66

job newsletter. These are all avenues through which you can spread the news of your new talent.

For instance, you can advertise yourself in the local newspaper. You may want to place an ad such as this:

> *Ventriloquist Available for Hire: Does Banquets,*
> *Birthday Parties, Special Events, etc.*
> *Contact John Doe at 555-5555*

Specialized papers also exist. Many organizations have newsletters or other mailings. If your profession has an information source such as these, it's a good opportunity for you to advertise yourself. Or if you are a Christian ventriloquist, for example, you can advertise in a denominational newspaper or magazine. Such an ad might look like the following:

> *Christian Ventriloquist Available for Hire:*
> *Does Bible Schools, Retreats, Revivals,*
> *Special Events, etc. —Fun for all ages.*
> *Contact John Doe at 555-5555*

Fliers

Not only are you surrounded by information sources, but you probably also receive a ton of junk mail every day. Yet "junk" mail is not always junk. As a ventriloquist you might want to send out fliers to advertise yourself. Send them to places where you would like to perform, or to places that might need you.

Let's begin by developing a flier for you. First, decide what is the size of the flier you want. If you're going to send a postcard, you'll need a lot less information than if you sent out an 8½″ ×11″ flier. Let's say, for example, that you want to use a standard size of paper for your mailing. Fliers of this size can have information on one side or both sides, and for mailing purposes they are usually folded into three sections.

If this is the type of flier that you want, get a piece of 8½″ ×11″ paper. Do you have your paper? Good. Now fold it lengthwise into three equal sections. Write in the different sections an idea of the information you want there.

Here are some suggestions about what to include in your flier:

1. A picture of you and your puppet(s)
2. A list of some of the places where you have performed
3. Some background information about yourself
4. Your fee or a suggested rate of pay if you charge one
5. A quotation from someone who has hired you in the past
6. And be sure to include how they can contact you!

Now you need to find a way to type or print the flier. Be sure to attach any clip art or pictures that might enhance the quality. Pictures usually print better if they are black-and-white, unless, of course, you are having a print shop develop your flier in color.

You must also decide how you want it printed. Do you want it on colored paper, pastel paper, or white paper? Choose a color that will enhance the flier. I have always preferred pastel colors because they're not so bright as to distract from the information, and yet they don't look as plain and standard as white. Of course, this is a personal preference. Choose the color that you want, but make sure that it looks professional.

Next you need to choose what bond, or weight, of paper to use. Although you don't need an extremely heavy bond, you will want something that is thick enough that the printing won't bleed through from the opposite side.

Finally you're ready to print the flier. Do you want the ink to be black, blue, red, etc.? Do you want different colors on the flier? Which of these options you choose will depend partly on how much money you desire to spend. Be careful not to make something so expensive that you don't want to send it out. You can develop a professional-looking flier for a minimal cost.

Talent Shows and Community Events

Talent shows and community events are two other ways to gain exposure. The more people see you perform, the more opportunities you will get to be seen. Opportunities will also come if a newspaper includes an article about you along with

an article about the talent show or the community event. Feel
free to send the papers a news release. For example, if you
win a talent show, write a short article about it and send it with
a picture to your local newspaper (most newspapers prefer a
black-and-white photo). If they're interested, you'll not only
be featured in an article, but the publicity won't cost you a
cent!

Talent Agencies

If you're interested in doing television commercials or
other large events, you should develop a professional portfolio and submit it to a talent agency. Most agencies like a portfolio of professional pictures showing you in various outfits and
situations. With it they require a résumé with basic information such as age, height, weight, eye color, address and phone
number. They also like to know your experience and your
hobbies. Before you develop a portfolio and résumé, however,
contact several agencies and have them send you information
concerning their requirements.

Word of Mouth

The best publicity is by word of mouth. When people
see you perform, they'll tell their friends. Then when their
friends have an event for which a ventriloquist could be useful, they'll call you. Where publicity is concerned, word of
mouth is your best friend (besides your partner, that is).

At this point you may want to develop a simple business
card—something that will serve as a reminder to anyone who
is interested or to anyone who may know someone who is interested in hiring you. The best advice concerning a business
card is to be creative. Feel free to be humorous. You may want
to put your puppet's picture on it or develop a catchy phrase
that will stick in people's minds.

The Follow-up Letter

Another good publicity technique is the follow-up letter.
Whenever you perform, send a brief, handwritten note the

next day to whomever hired you, saying how much you enjoyed the event. Again put your talents at their disposal. Let them know that you are available whenever they need you. This technique will keep you fresh in their minds.

There are three important ideas to keep in mind while writing a follow-up letter:

1. Be courteous
2. Be brief and to the point
3. Include your address and phone number at the bottom of the letter

The follow-up letter is not only a polite way to respond to having had the opportunity to perform, it is a way to make you distinct in the recipient's mind. Your employer will most likely be flattered that you took the time to write and will be impressed by your courtesy. The letter will set you apart from other performers who have not responded similarly, will help establish a rapport between you and the person who hired you and will provide once again your address and telephone number, which you can never do too frequently. For something that only takes a few minutes to write, the follow-up letter can prove to be a very effective way to promote yourself as a ventriloquist.

Review

These are just a few of the ways you can market your new talent. Put an ad in the newspaper, a newsletter or a specialized magazine. Develop a flier. Become involved in talent shows or other community events. Submit a portfolio to a local talent agency. Design a business card and pass it out liberally. Let people know that you're ready and willing to perform. Send a follow-up letter after every performance. Find ways to put yourself at your employers' disposal—to keep you fresh in their minds.

A good motto for publicity is "The squeaky wheel gets the oil." In other words, the more you squeak, the more attention you'll get. The more you gain public exposure, the more opportunities you will have to perform. So go make yourself known. Don't wait for them to come to you—you go to them.

14. Scheduling Shows

Picture this scene. It's about seven in the evening. You're home from work, watching television. Suddenly the phone rings.

"Oh, no. Another salesman," you say.

You meander to the phone and reluctantly answer, "Hello."

"Is (*your name*) there?"

"This is he/she."

"I hear that you are a ventriloquist and I was wondering if you would be interested in . . ."

Congratulations! You've just experienced your first professional phone call as a ventriloquist.

"But wait! What do I say? What do I ask?"

That's the purpose of this chapter: To prepare you for that first, on-the-spot phone call that will probably come when you least expect it.

The Questions

To begin with, whenever you are scheduling a show, the same rule applies as when you are at the show: in all that you say and do, present yourself as a professional. Even if you don't feel like a professional, as the guest performer you must present yourself to the best of your ability.

With that important key in mind, be courteous when someone asks you to perform. Being courteous doesn't mean that you don't ask questions: you will need some important information to be properly prepared for the program. There are some basic questions that you always should ask. You don't have to memorize them. Most of them are common sense and you would probably ask them anyway, but preparation as a professional is never in vain.

Here are some questions to become familiar with:

1. How long do you want my program to be?
2. What type of audience will be there (i.e., children, youths, senior citizens, etc.)?
3. Does the program have a theme?

71

4. Where will the program be held? (If you don't know the location, ask for specific directions to the site of the program.)
5. What time will the program begin?
6. What time should I arrive?
7. How should I dress?
8. What is the name and phone number of the person to whom I am talking (i.e., the contact person)?

Being prepared to ask these questions on the spot is better than forgetting them and having to call back later. Or worse yet, what if you don't get the information you need and you forget to get the name and number of the person who called you? How do you know where to go? Or when to arrive? How can you be properly prepared?

I once forgot to ask the name of the person who invited me to perform. I arrived the day of the program not knowing what was going on and having to ask "Who's in charge here?" It was very embarrassing.

In addition to this, when you're talking to the contact person you should not make a commitment to do anything until you have checked your calendar. Over the past thirteen years and through more than 600 performances I have only canceled one performance, and that was due to illness. Nor have I ever been late. If you make a commitment, if you say that you are going to be somewhere at a certain time, you need to be true to your word. Once you say yes, there's no turning back.

Canceling performances gives you a bad reputation. If people can't rely on you to be there, they'll find someone that they can rely on. My motto is "Never cancel." If you're sick and can still do ventriloquism, stick to your commitment.

Of course, also use common sense. If you're contagious or your symptoms might affect your performance, then common sense would suggest that you should cancel it. But only cancel under extreme circumstances, and, if you must cancel, give the contact person a personal phone call as soon as possible. Don't leave a message with a spouse, believing that the matter is settled, and don't persuade someone else to call for you. Keep calling until you reach the contact and then personally explain the situation. As soon as you are well, send a card apologizing for any inconvenience that you may have caused, and let the person know that you would love to come at a future date.

Calling the week before the program to confirm the show and the time to be there is also a good habit to form. This is a good opportunity to ask any last-minute questions. Some places will send you a confirmation letter a few days in advance, but most won't. Once I called the day before an event and the contact person told me, "Oh, I haven't had a chance to get a hold of you. We canceled it."

Always be prepared. Become familiar with the questions listed above and with any other basic information that you may wish to know. For instance, some performers like to ask if a sound system will be available. If you are planning to use a music tape during your performance, ask if they have access to a tape player. And remember, always be courteous. Be a professional from the first "Hello" to the last "Good-bye."

15. The Big Day

It's D Day. Or perhaps I should say "P Day." That is, it's "Performance Day," the day that you've been anxiously awaiting. Hopefully this chapter will help to relieve any tension you might be feeling. There is no reason to be nervous. If you have been prepared in practice, you'll be prepared when you walk onstage. Of course, if you have scoffed every time you read "Practice, practice, practice," and marked it out with your pen rather than highlighting it—then you might want to go sit in a corner and chew your fingernails. Remember: unless you're at a ventriloquist convention, you're probably the only one in the room. That makes you the best!

Nevertheless, here are several keys that will help you to be prepared when the big day arrives:

First, plan ahead and don't be late. Allow plenty of time to arrive, with time to spare. Locate the place of your performance in advance. Dress your vent figure in the proper clothes the night before, and make a list of the props you will need. Performing is very difficult if you arrive and realize that your puppet is still at home. If you are using a tape, cue it to the right place. If you ever forget an item, be creative. The audience doesn't know that you've forgotten it. Be inventive and improvise. Of course, you always benefit from proper preparation.

Second, make a good first impression. The old saying says "You never get a second chance to make a good first impression." Enter poised and with a smile. Be prepared to shake anyone's hand, and when you do, shake it firmly. Don't slouch. Stand up straight and be polite. Courtesy pays.

If you get a chance, talk to the people who will be operating the sound system. Give them any instructions or background music tapes that you might be using, and, if you have time, practice with the microphone.

Sometimes before I perform, I walk around the perimeter of the room to help myself prepare for the audience. This allows me to see from the point of view of the people who will be watching the dialogue. It reveals to me how large the room is and how wide the audience will be on my left and right.

As the time for your moment in the spotlight arrives, you will find yourself backstage. When I first began, this was the most difficult time for me. I couldn't see the audience, and my imagination would run wildly through horrible scenarios. Waiting is always difficult, but use this time to bring your figure to life. Talk with him and carry through with a conversation. Having him be alive beforehand will help you to keep him alive as you walk onto the stage. You might even find someone to talk to, a child or a backstage volunteer, but remember, your puppet should be alive from the moment your hand enters it—even if you are all alone.

If you've practiced thoroughly, then there's no need to review the script while backstage. I completely avoid it. I find that many times when I try to hurriedly review parts of a dialogue in my mind, I usually make mistakes. If you're backstage and preparing to perform, this won't help you. It will only lower your confidence level and distract you.

Suddenly you're introduced. Your time has come. Go out and enjoy yourself. Don't worry, everything will fall into place. If you've practiced and prepared, your dialogue will flow naturally.

Walk out with confidence. Here's an opportunity to make a good first impression, and the first thirty seconds of your dialogue will set the tone for the remainder of the program.

As you perform, make an effort to establish eye contact with the audience. In other words, don't hide from them and don't be afraid to look at them. After all, you're not the dummy. It would be a shame if he made more eye contact than you did.

Eye contact will include the audience in your dialogue. Looking at them eye to eye makes them feel like a part of the program. Be sure that you don't neglect a certain part of the auditorium: both you and your puppet should look at them from front to back, far left to far right. Include everyone and, when you talk, project your voice as if you were speaking to the person in the back row.

As the dialogue ends and you leave the stage, keep your figure alive. He should never be dead on your hand. Even after the audience can no longer see you, the figure should remain alive and talking. Have him say a few words to you or someone else before putting him "to sleep." By keeping him alive you will maintain the illusion of his reality both for yourself and for anyone else who may be watching.

Finally, remember that your time onstage is *your* time onstage. No one is going to take it from you. While you're onstage, you have the floor, and no one will take it from you until you say that magic word, "Good-bye."

The people in the audience are there to see you. You are there to entertain. They want to have a good time. You want to have a good time. Go out and have a good time with them. Relax and enjoy making people laugh.

But remember, before you walk out the door on that big day, there are some items you need to bring with you:

1. Your vent figure(s)
2. Your stand
3. Any tapes that you may be using
4. Any props that you may be using
5. Directions to the event
6. The contact person's phone number in case you have car problems or get lost

16. What Would *You* Do?

Life doesn't always go the way you expect it. Likewise, performances don't always go the way you plan them. Mistakes and accidents may and will happen, but don't give up. Keep an optimistic attitude and learn to expect the unexpected.

That's the topic of this chapter, the unexpected, but please understand its purpose. It is not to promote the idea that you should imagine the worst happening, nor is it to make you afraid. The aim of this chapter is to give you some experience in handling situations before you ever step onto a stage. These situations shouldn't scare you. Instead they should make you more confident that if anything out of the ordinary should happen, you'll be prepared. That way you won't have to fear the unexpected, and perhaps you can even turn it to your good.

In the next few pages I am going to place you into the spotlight of some interesting experiences. Read each situation. Then place yourself in the shoes of the ventriloquist. Stop and imagine how you would handle the situation. Then read how I have or would have handled it.

Situation #1: You have just walked onstage. You place your figure on his stand but notice that something doesn't look quite right. As you begin your dialogue you realize the problem: someone adjusted the microphone to the wrong height. Oh no! Adjusting a microphone takes two hands, and one of yours is *very* occupied at the moment. If it leaves, the vent figure dies—literally. What do you do?

Solution: First of all, don't panic. It's no big deal. Just stop your dialogue and ask someone who is in charge to help you. It's all right to ask someone to do something for you, and they won't say no. There's no reason to apologize to the audience. They understand your dilemma.

Instead, look for an opportunity to turn the circumstances to your benefit. For instance, after the person adjusts the problem, you might want to follow with a quick joke, such as:

VENTRILOQUIST (*To the person who helped you*): Thank you very much. (*To the vent figure*) I like people like that. You know,

77

people like that don't grow on trees.
FIGURE: Yeah, they *hang* from them.

Or:

VENTRILOQUIST (*To the person who helped you*): Thank you very
much. I would give you a hand, (*look at the vent figure*) but
I've already given him one.

Then continue with your skit. By making the situation
funny, you've turned a small inconvenience into a great advantage. The audience has already sympathized with your situation, laughed at your unexpected humor, and you haven't
even begun your dialogue. What an entrance!

Of course, be sure to use selective humor, especially when
you direct a joke toward a person. If you know that you are
going to make a humorous remark about a specific person in
the audience, always go to that person beforehand and ask
for permission. And if you make an off-the-cuff remark such
as the first example above, always go to the person immedi-
ately following the program and make sure that you caused
no offense.

Situation #2: While you are performing, a young child moves
forward and stands one foot in front of you, staring at you.
What do you do? How would you tactfully handle this situation?

Solution: There's no one, set answer for any of these situations, especially for this one. Much of your response will depend on the audience. Learn to read their faces. How are
they responding? Is the kid distracting them? And what kind
of performance is this? Is it serious? Formal? Relaxed?

Sometimes it's best just to ignore the child. He's not really
interfering with the show: he just decided to find a closer seat.
Don't bring more attention to him, and it's really best not to
make any jokes about him.

In addition, the audience might think it's cute. If he stands
there for a while, you might even have your vent figure look
down and say, "Oh, hello there," and then continue with your

dialogue. Sometimes the child will leave if you do this, but if he continues to watch from his front-row seat, one foot in front of you, have your vent figure look at him occasionally. After all, he is part of the audience too.

Situation #3: You're onstage. You're in the middle of your script and suddenly . . . you go blank. You forget your line. What do you do? What can you do?

Solution: Don't panic. Your natural desire will be to freeze. *Don't go silent.* Don't freeze up. Don't say, "Oh no! I forgot my line." That's honest, but it's not very professional. Don't say, "Ahhhhhhh . . . I knew I should have practiced more." Or, "Whoops. I forgot where I was."

The first year I began performing, I had not yet learned to apply the number one rule of ventriloquism: practice, practice, practice. I was performing a script that I had memorized two days earlier. I wasn't ready and I forgot my lines. I froze. Silence fell upon the room as I turned different shades of red. I quickly remembered the script, but it was too late. They knew it and I knew it. I had blown it.

Sometimes when you forget a line you can just skip over it or pass on to the next joke without sacrificing the theme or quality of the script. If so, then continue forward. Remember, the audience doesn't know your script, and they don't know when you've forgotten a line, so the best solution is to keep going without missing a beat.

But if you can't, then turn to an alternative. Ad-lib. To ad-lib means to keep talking, making the dialogue up as you go. The audience will never know that you made a mistake, and, as you talk, you allow yourself time to remember your line and to return to your original dialogue.

Another option is to have your vent figure interrupt you and say:

FIGURE: Hey, let's sing a song.
VENTRILOQUIST: But we were talking.
F: Yeah, but I want to sing. Please? Please?
V: Well, okay, but let's make it quick.

Then have him sing some song that you know. You might even include the audience. Let them sing with your puppet. Then when he's done you can return to your dialogue.

Or you could enter into a series of short jokes about being hungry. Your figure could interrupt you and say:

F: Hey! I'm HUNGRY!!!!!
V: You can't be.
F: Why not?
V: I gave you your supper.
F: Yeah. Spinach!
V: What's wrong with spinach? It'll put color in your cheeks.
F: Sure, but who wants green cheeks?

From here you can bring the conversation back to the original dialogue without anyone knowing that you departed from it.

Most of all, if you forget your lines, keep talking: if silence falls, the audience will really know you made a mistake. And don't let your vent figure go limp: keep him moving and don't let him die. After all, it's not *his* fault.

Of course, rather than covering a mistake, the best method is to avoid making them. By now you should know how. It's the first and last rule of ventriloquism: practice, practice, practice.

Situation #4: Your moment on stage has finally come. You step out. Every eye is on you. You gracefully walk to your vent stand. Your figure is alive. You begin the routine, and suddenly a two-year-old child becomes frightened by your puppet. He starts to cry and say, "Mommy. I want my mommy." He's making noise and, rather than taking him out of the room, his mother is trying to convince him that it's just a puppet. While this is happening, you realize that the baby is receiving more attention than you. What do you do?

Solution: In a situation like this, you can't stop. Although the entire audience is distracted, keep going. Keep moving. As the child becomes quiet, their attention will return to you, but don't stop and wait for this. Just put the distraction out of your mind. You can't do anything to change the circumstances, and stopping or making a comment about it would only embarrass the mom. Since you can't change the situation, you'll just have to live with it and bear it until you win back the audience's attention.

Situation #5: In the middle of your dialogue you hear someone say, "His lips are moving." How embarrassing! Suddenly you feel about as small as a mouse. Do you shorten your routine? Should you quit early? What would you do?

Solution: Did you choose to quit early? I hope not. First, realize that just because someone makes the comment "His lips are moving," it doesn't necessarily mean that your lips really are moving. And perhaps they did move. So what? Big deal. So your lips moved *once.*

On the other hand, perhaps your lips didn't move at all and the person who made this statement did it to get attention. Or perhaps he saw your throat move. Anyone can speak without moving his lips, but no one can speak without moving his throat. It's unavoidable.

"In that case, I'll wear a turtleneck sweater."

As I mentioned before, if you try to hide the fact that your throat moves when your figure speaks, you'll only attract more attention to it.

Finally, if you ever hear a comment like this from the audience or even from someone after the show— "Hey, I saw your lips moving"—don't let it hinder you from continuing to do ventriloquism. Put it behind you and try not to give it a second thought. Most of all, never dwell on these negative remarks.

I almost quit ventriloquism once. I was no more than a beginner and was performing at a youth activity in my church. I was a youth myself, and several hundred of my peers were in the room. I was in front of them all and they loved it—except for a young lady who was a good friend of mine. She didn't even look at me. She seemed so embarrassed—embarrassed for me. I never asked her if this was truly what she was feeling, but the damage was done. When I finished, I was crushed. I said to myself, "I'll never do this again—not if I'm going to embarrass my friends and make a fool out of myself."

Then another thought occurred to me: "No. I won't quit. I'll become better. I'll become so good that no one will be embarrassed for me."

When you face an adverse situation, a rude comment, a hurtful look, and you want to quit, you can do one of two things: (1) you can quit, or (2) you can face the situation and become better because of it. Having been there myself, I would advise the second option.

Learn to expect the unexpected. Someday it will happen to you. It has happened to me. Once I was performing a magic trick outside. During the trick I held a cape in front of my vent figure's head. Suddenly from out of nowhere there came a huge gust of wind. It blew aside the cape and revealed the secret of the trick. What do you do? What can you do except to keep going as if it never happened?

Another time I was performing a levitating trick with my vent figure, and the "trick" table on which I had laid him began to fall. Henry, my partner, almost took the dive of his life. I had to catch both him and the table and fix the problem while continuing my dialogue. I quickly left my script and began to ad-lib, which became the most humorous part of the evening.

Fortunately such circumstances are rare. A clear majority of your programs will be problem-free, but it's always good to be prepared. You never know when you might come face to face with the unexpected, and if you make mistakes, don't quit. There's no reason to punish yourself. Tomorrow is a new day, and next week is a new program with a new audience. Look upon the situations you face as learning experiences.

17. Record-Keeping

Once I was the "special feature" at the vacation bible school of a large church. I had a great time. The children had a great time. The church said, "We want you to come back in the future."

A year passed. Two years passed, and then one day the phone rang.

"Can you come be the special feature at our vacation bible school this year?"

They wanted me to come back. So I said, "Sure. I'll be there. No problem."

No problem? No problem! There was a big problem. Two years earlier I had neglected to write down which scripts I had performed. Some of the children would be the same kids, and kids have good memories.

I tried to guess which ones I had performed—I was wrong. They had already seen some of it. As one person pointed out to me, "I think you did that skit better this time than you did two years ago." I was embarrassed. They still enjoyed it, but I should have been more prepared. I should have kept better records.

Records? What Records?

As you perform more, more places will begin to ask you to return. This presents a problem. You don't want to perform the same dialogues in the same places. You don't want to tell the same jokes, but your last performance there was a year ago and you can't remember which dialogues you did.

Good record-keeping is a great way to avoid this problem. Beginning with your first ventriloquist program, keep a log or a diary. Then whenever you perform, write down important information concerning that program.

A good ventriloquist's record-keeping book contains eight important pieces of information:

1. *The program number* (Is it your first or your three-hundred-and-first program?)

2. *The place or organization* (Who was the program for?)
3. *The contact person's name* (Who contacted you about doing this program?)
4. *The phone number and address of the contact* (How do you contact this person?)
5. *The date* (When was the program performed?)
6. *The scripts* (Which dialogues did you perform? Give each script a one- or two-letter name.)
7. *Puppet names* (Which puppets did you use?)
8. *Other notes that you may wish to remember* (This last note includes anything that you may wish to remember if they ask you to return. For example, was it a special occasion? Were they a good audience? Did they have a bad sound system? Were you in a crowded room? Did they have a tape player? And so forth.)

Organization

Record-keeping is great—that is, if you can find your records when you need them. As far as your performance log is concerned, organization is of paramount importance. If you aren't organized with your records, your records will do you no good.

"Oh no. But I'm no good at organizing!"

Don't worry. You don't have to be a greatly organized person to be a great ventriloquist. (Although it would help you in this chapter!)

You can catalog information in a number of effective ways. The easiest method is to keep your records in a notebook. A notebook allows you quick access to any part of the record at any moment. You may wish to organize it as in the following examples:

1. The John Doe Charitable Organization
   John Doe——555-5555——3/9/96
   School / Love is Forever——Andy the Monkey
   Notes: Sweethearts' Banquet——Bad Sound System

2. Public School System
   John Smith——555-5556——3/15/96

School / Math / Song——Andy the Monkey & Henry
Notes: Academic Pep Rally

3. First Baptist Church
   Jane Doe——555-5557——3/18/96
   Song / David & Goliath / Jesus Loves Me——Henry
   Notes: Children's Party——Good Audience / No
       Tape Player

The advantage of using this system is that your programs are listed in chronological order. But although this system is the easiest to organize and although it catalogs your performances in chronological order, it does have its limitations. For example, when you do a second performance for a certain organization, the program will be listed elsewhere in your record book.

Another method of record-keeping that may be more suitable is the card-catalog system. After each performance cite the important information on a note card and keep it in a card holder. This system will allow plenty of room for notes and other information concerning repeat performances. Then organize the file according to the organization or place name.

Examine the following example which lists two performances, one in March and one in June, for the same organization on the same information card.

> *Program # 13 The John Doe Charitable Organization*
> *John Doe——555-5555——3/9/96*
> *School / Love is Forever——Andy the Monkey*
> *Notes: Sweethearts' Banquet——Bad Sound System*

> *Program # 54 Repeat Performance——6/12/97*
> *Hungry / Song / Magic Trick——Henry*
> *Notes: None*

Don't Lose It!

Always keep your record book in the same place. I have a shelf devoted solely to my ventriloquism dialogue books, joke books, ventriloquism tapes and my performance record-keeping book. This diary is one jewel that you don't want to lose, not only for the sake of information, but also for the sake of memories. In time when you thumb through your record book, you will see performances that you don't even remember. Others will make you laugh. Some may even make you blush, but whatever the emotion, years from now you will wish you had kept good records.

Final Word

Above all, find a method of record-keeping that is organized, one that will allow you quick and easy access and that is suited to meet your needs. When I first began doing ventriloquism I also kept a scrap book. In this I included newspaper articles, ribbons, promotional fliers and anything else I considered to be special. You may want to incorporate this into your record-keeping book.

However you decide to keep records, one matter is sure—if you don't keep good records from the beginning, you'll regret it later.

18. Uses of Ventriloquism

Ventriloquism amazes people of all ages. In a matter of moments a lifeless puppet can become real and talk to them. With senior citizens in rest homes, children in preschool and every age in between I have witnessed the laughter that a puppet can bring.

"How do you 'throw' your voice? How can you talk without moving your lips?"

I have yet to meet a person who isn't amused or intrigued by the art. I have yet to meet a person who doesn't enjoy laughing. Nevertheless, ventriloquism can be more than a tool to make people laugh. It can be a profound teaching tool. Professionals can use the art in many fields.

The Dentist Ventriloquist

Imagine a young child who has never been to the dentist's office. His first checkup time has come. His mom has made an appointment, and like any child facing a new experience, he's nervous. He doesn't know the dentist. He's never seen a dentist. He doesn't even know what a dentist is! What is the dentist going to say? What is he going to do? The child's fears are natural. Yet, when he arrives, not only is he introduced to the dentist, but to a dentist puppet as well, perhaps even a tooth puppet. Before long he has a new friend. Some children will even look forward to returning because they know they'll see the puppet again.

The Doctor Ventriloquist

Doctors can use ventriloquism in a wide variety of ways. Puppets can be used to make a new patient feel comfortable. They can be used to help explain a physical problem that the child is having. They would also make great visitors to a child who has just had surgery or who has had an extended hospital stay. They can even be used during a typical examination.

The Police Ventriloquist

A policeman can use ventriloquism as a means of promoting awareness about a topic. He and his vent figure can educate children about the dangers of drugs and criminal actions. Perhaps he could visit a class or a school once a month: that way the children would become familiar with both the policeman and his puppet. They would look forward to his coming and could learn important lessons about obeying the law and respecting authority. Overall, ventriloquism is both a great teaching and a great public relations tool.

Beyond the classroom and the school atmosphere, ventriloquism is also useful when working with children who are the victims of crime. Following a traumatic incident some children tend to close up—they don't want to talk about what has happened, and an adult questioning them can be intimidating. Adults are so much larger than children, but a puppet is not. A puppet, in a manner of speaking, is on their level. Some children would open up to a puppet quicker than they would to an adult.

I have heard of foot policemen who carry puppets with them on their assigned routes. The whole neighborhood quickly comes to know such a policeman, beginning with the children and their parents. The puppet helps to build a rapport with the people, a great benefit to the policeman as he continues to walk that route.

The Fireman Ventriloquist

The fireman ventriloquist, like his counterpart above, can use ventriloquism in many ways. Imagine a classroom visiting the fire station and suddenly Joe the Fireman Puppet appears and teaches the children what to do if they are ever on fire.

"Stop, drop and roll," he says, before leading them in a "Fireman" song.

This is another example of how a puppet can be used to teach important lessons. Firemen can also use ventriloquism to help children who have just experienced a tragic situation.

The School Ventriloquist

Puppets can be used by teachers in the classroom, especially in elementary schools. Imagine a George Washington puppet who teaches about the Revolutionary War. Or an Abraham Lincoln puppet who teaches about the Civil War. Picture an old lady puppet who teaches the children addition and subtraction.

In elementary-school classrooms puppets can be very useful: that is, they can be useful so long as they are not overused. The appearance of a puppet needs to be a special treat, not a daily routine.

Another use for a school ventriloquist is in the area of counseling. When I was in elementary school we had a counselor who wasn't a ventriloquist but who used a puppet. It was a dolphin puppet, and although the counselor's lips moved when the puppet spoke, it was a very effective tool to teach us to look both ways before crossing the street and not to talk to strangers, etc. She came to our class once a month, and her visits were always a special treat.

The Church Ventriloquist

Ventriloquism in the church can be used for children's parties, retreats, camps, vacation bible schools, church banquets, revivals and so forth. The puppet can teach people of all ages about God's love. He can tell Bible stories and teach moral truths and make them laugh in the process. As with any vocation, the uses of ventriloquism in the church are innumerable.

Ventriloquism can be a profound benefit to almost any field of work, especially for those who work with children. Of course, people of all ages love ventriloquism, and professionals can use the art in virtually any field. The dentist and the doctor can use the art in working with new children or in helping a child understand a problem. Police officers can use ventriloquism to teach about drugs or the dangers of drinking and driving. Counselors can use puppets in their work with children. In hospitals, churches, nursing homes, social work—the possibilities are endless. Whether you're a police-man, a teacher, a car salesman or a secretary—in whatever profession you may work, look for opportunities to use your puppet to make someone else's day brighter.

The world needs more ventriloquists. The world needs more laughter, and many times people will listen to a "dummy" quicker than they will listen to a real person.

About the Author

Picture a fourth grade class. The teacher is teaching. The students are listening—or so it seems. Little do they know that one of their students is talking—without seeming to speak.

That's how Kolby King began ventriloquism. After seeing a Christian ventriloquist at his church and telling himself, "I can do that," he began trying to talk in class without moving his lips. Jokingly his parents bought him a book about ventriloquism and a monkey puppet. A year later he began performing, placing first in his school's fifth-grade talent show.

Now more than thirteen years later and after more than 600 performances, Kolby has performed across Oklahoma and into the surrounding states. Performing as many as 100 times a year, he has helped with numerous charitable causes and has placed in both state and regional talent competitions.

But, in 1988 Kolby's ventriloquist career took a different direction:

> "I used to love performing just as entertainment, but I noticed that when I left, the laughter left also. Then Jesus Christ changed my life. He gave me a reason to live and a message to share. Since that time I have devoted my talents to telling people about His love."

Kolby King is currently a minister in Oklahoma City.

"Wait a minute!~ Wait a minute!" interrupts Henry, one of Kolby's vent figures. "What about me?"
"What about you?"
"Don't I get to say something?"
Sure."
"I just want everyone to know that Kolby has a big heart."
"Thanks, Henry."
"And a big stomach to match."

Recommended Resources

For information regarding

1. ventriloquist dialogues
2. puppets, vent figures and other ventriloquism equipment
3. a professional ventriloquist home-study course
4. The North American Association of Ventriloquists

contact:

Maher Ventriloquist Studios
P.O. Box 420
Littleton, CO 80160
(303) 798-6830

An additional resource for puppets is:

Axtell Expressions, Inc.
230 Glencrest Circle
Ventura, CA 93003
(805) 642-7282
E-mail: expressions@axtell.com
Internet: http://www.axtell.com